Bible Stuff

Spiritual Teaching for Under Fives that's Fun

God Gives us Families
Here Comes Christmas!

Janet Gaukroger

Contents

God gives us Families

Here comes Christmas!

Introduction

Welcome to *Bible Stuff* – an activity-based curriculum designed to help us communicate spiritual truth to children from birth to age five.

Basic beliefs

There's no doubt that children take in a massive amount of information in the first five years of their lives. Many significant attitudes and habits are formed which will last a lifetime. It is so important that we pass on the Christian faith to our children from the very beginning. We have the opportunity to give them a heritage of spiritual strength. *Bible Stuff* is one attempt to help us make the most of that opportunity by combining a number of factors to produce an effective programme. The programme's four basic beliefs are as follows.

1. Communicating Biblical truth is very important

Bible Stuff is committed to the truth and accuracy of the Bible as God's Word, living and active in today's world. Teaching it to the next generation is a serious responsibility.

2. Teaching in ways that under fives can understand is crucial

We have not effectively taught the Bible if the recipients of our teaching have not learned. We must, therefore, understand where under fives are in their physical, mental, spiritual and emotional development so that we can teach in ways they will relate to.

3. Children learn through play

Recognizing that play is the child's work means choosing activities that are fun, but that are also part of the development process.

4. Children are all different

Providing a variety of activities simultaneously allows a child to express his or her own personality by choosing what to be involved in. (*Bible Stuff* does not recommend everybody doing the same thing at the same time. It recognizes that one child may be happy to play in the home corner for an entire session, and another child may need the stimulation of four or five different things in the same period of time.)

This curriculum has been tried and tested by the under fives teachers at Stopsley Baptist Church in Luton. I owe them a great deal for their loyalty and support over many years.

May God envision, encourage and empower us through his Holy Spirit as we 'tell the next generation the praiseworthy deeds of the Lord' (Psalm 78:4).

How to use this book

Bible Stuff contains two teaching units, one of five weeks and one of four. The story and activities for each week are completely self-contained, though spending four or five weeks on the same theme reinforces the teaching. For each session you will find:

Preparation

This includes Bible background or a meditation for teachers – we need to feed on God's word ourselves in order to teach effectively.

Story Time

This section includes a short selection of Bible verses related to the theme of the session. They are paraphrased in language under fives can understand. Use them throughout the session as you talk to and with the babies and children. The more they hear us saying 'The Bible says...', the more they will learn what a special book it is.

✏️ Teaching Activities

These are divided into activities for babies, toddlers, 2s – 3s and 3s – 5s. Again, if your class combines ages, choose an activity from each age group. You will find that some of them overlap.

👥 Group Time

There are separate suggestions for 2s – 3s and 3s – 5s. If you are working with babies and toddlers, sitting them all down at once to hear the story is rarely a possibility. Don't worry – you can be telling them parts of the story all through the session. In fact, you can do that with all under fives, so that when they hear the story in group time, it will have a familiar ring.

Take Home!

Each session ends with a photocopiable take-home paper. This is to give to parents or carers and is designed so that they can follow up the teaching at home. It gives the story and Bible verses, then two or three suggestions for home-based activities, at least one of which is suitable for babies. You may need to give some explanation and encouragement to the parents / carers to help them make the most of the take-home sheet.

Planning

Start by reading through the whole unit: some activities require the collection of various items in advance. Also, teachers can share responsibility for bringing any necessary equipment. Some activities are suggested for more than one age group, so if you have more than one class of under fives, co-ordination between groups will help all concerned.

Setting up

If possible, try to have the room ready when children arrive. This creates a more relaxed atmosphere. You do not need a lot of fancy equipment or expensive toys. For under fives, bricks, a simple home corner, puzzles and books should be available at every session. They give a sense of continuity and are also the most-used items for this age group. Don't put out all of your equipment each time you meet. Using the activities suggested for each week adds variety. Look through them to make a basic equipment list.

Group time

Group time comes at the end of each session and is an important part of the teaching / learning process, but it is not the only part. It's to be hoped that teaching will be going on throughout the session in the various activities. Group time should be between five and ten minutes long, depending on the age and maturity level of the children. Its components are conversation, singing, prayer, telling the Bible story and sometimes a 'game' or 'activity'. The order of these components can vary from session to session. Try to choose the moment when the children are most settled to tell the story. Sometimes some of the children may want to pray, sometimes only a teacher will pray. You may find that you need to sing four or five songs to settle children, and another time it will only take one. Try to have several ideas ready for group time, but remain flexible.

Health and safety

Never leave children unsupervised when using sand, water and dough. If necessary, put these items out of reach until you can come back to them. If you are in any doubt about mess, cover the children's clothing with aprons. If you are not sure about safety guidelines, ask someone who is. Check with your local social services office, get information from your local library or make contact with the person responsible for health and safety in your church building.

Resources

The following books offer detailed help and information:

Sharing Jesus with Under Fives, Janet Gaukroger, Crossway Books
Children in Crèches and Toddler Groups, Ann Croft, CPAS

God Gives us Families   Week 1

THE FIRST FAMILY (GENESIS 1 - 4)

Aim To help the children understand that God made families; that families were God's idea.

Preparation

Today's story is taken from the first few chapters of Genesis. The creation of the first family does not appear in the Bible as a narrative. The scriptures don't tell it neatly for us! We put the story together as we read the whole account of creation.

The idea of relationship was there from the beginning. The relationship between Adam and Eve was God's idea. He was the one who said, 'It is not good for man to be alone.' It was God who said that a man and a woman would leave their parents and become one together. It was God who told them to be fruitful and multiply.

Although Adam and Eve did not have children until after they had sinned and been expelled from the garden, producing a family had clearly been God's intention for them. Their family life was no fairy story - even in the first family there was the jealousy and rivalry we see between our children today. Can't you hear Cain saying, 'It's not fair! Abel's sacrifice wasn't any better than mine.'? Some things never change!

But, despite their failures, we see in Adam and Eve and their family the beginning of God's plan for men, women and children.

How can this encourage us? We all have struggles as we work out our own family lives. Husband-wife relationships are not always perfect; children are often a blessing, but sometimes an immense frustration. But despite the difficulties, God's original perfect plan was for men and women who love each other to be joined in marriage and have families. Our personal lives should reflect his image, and so should our family relationships. Let's be encouraged that even in the problems we face, God is on our side, longing through the power of the Holy Spirit to restore us - and our relationships - to his image.

What do we want to communicate to the children? We want to help them understand that God planned for people to live in families. Of course, with some of the children, we need to be sensitive to the particular definition of family that they know. We recognize that many people today do not live in homes where a mother and father bring up their own children and contact with their wider family may be limited. God loves each family represented among our children, even if its make-up does not reflect his plan. We want to communicate that love and care.

It is so easy for children to pick up negative feelings about family life, even from an early age. Our aim is to present children with a positive and joyful attitude to families in general, and their own family in particular.

'Lord, as I try to communicate to the children your love and care for families, please help me to be thankful for my own family. Where there are problems, please help me to have new wisdom this week, and the peace that comes from you. Where there are joys, help me to praise you. As I teach this week, please help me to make the most of opportunities for conversation with the children. Amen.'

Story Time

Bible verses
God looked at everything he made and it was very good. (Genesis 1:31)
God made a man and a woman. (Genesis 1:27)
God cares for you. (1 Peter 5:7)
God planned for families. (Genesis 2:24)

Birth - 2s

A long time ago God made the first family. God made a man. His name was Adam. Adam looked after the plants and animals God had made. God did not want Adam to be alone. So he made a woman. Her name was Eve. Adam and Eve lived in the beautiful world God had made.

God planned for Adam and Eve to have children. They had a baby boy. His name was Cain. After a while they had another baby. His name was Abel. Adam and Eve and their children were the first family.

3s - 5s

A long time ago God made the first family. God made a man. His name was Adam. Adam lived by himself in the beautiful world God had made. He gave names to all the different kinds of animals. Adam was lonely, though, because he was the only person that God had made.

God did not want Adam to be lonely. So he made a woman. Her name was Eve. Adam loved Eve. They enjoyed all the things that God had made. They ate fruits and vegetables from the trees and plants.

God planned for Adam and Eve to have children. They had a baby boy. His name was Cain. Adam and Eve took care of Cain. After a while they had another baby. His name was Abel. Adam and Eve and their children were the first family.

Teaching Activities

In all activities this morning, take every opportunity to talk about families - tell parts of the Bible story, talk about each child's family and about God's care for families.

Babies

Look at books about families Two or three board books with simple, clear pictures will be enough. You may want to read the text aloud, or just talk to a baby about the pictures. Alternatively, make your own book about families. Cut out about six pictures of families and individuals of different ages from magazines or catalogues. Glue each picture on a separate piece of lightweight card. Punch holes along the left-hand side and tie the pages together with ribbon or wool. If you want, you can print a simple sentence on each page: for example, 'Thank you, God, for families'; 'Some families have big brothers and sisters'; 'It is fun to go to Grandma's house'.

Feel fruits and vegetables Bring three or four colourful, robust fruits or vegetables for the babies to look at and feel. Marrows, carrots, apples, courgettes and oranges would all be suitable. As the babies feel the different shapes and textures, and see the variety of colours, you can talk about Adam and Eve eating fruits and vegetables. As you tell part of the story you can emphasize God's plan for Adam and Eve, and his care for them.

Bring a box to explore Obtain a large cardboard box for the babies to climb in and out of. Apple boxes are usually very strong and are about the right size. Most large supermarkets have a good supply of empty boxes. Check for any protruding staples. For younger babies who are just starting to move, turn the box on its side. Let babies who are more confident in movement climb in, out and over the box. This activity does not relate directly to today's theme, but it provides opportunities to talk to babies about how God planned for them to grow, and about the enjoyable things we can do at church.

Toddlers

Bring one or two boxes for toddlers to explore today. Bring fruits and vegetables for them to look at and touch. You may also wish to consider some of the following activities.

Glue a mural of families Provide several pictures of family members of different ages, sexes and races. Mail-order catalogues are a good source of such pictures, though they rarely feature older people: magazines may be a better source of such pictures. Bring a large, long sheet of plain paper onto which the children may glue their pictures. Attach it to the wall at child height, or allow the children to work on the floor. You may want to write, 'God Made Families' across the top. As the children glue pictures, there will be opportunities for conversations about the Bible story, or about their own families. At the end of the session display the mural where the parents can see it when they come to collect their children. Older toddlers may want to show their pictures to their parents.

Cooking, and laying the table Replace the usual home corner equipment with a few small saucepans from a real kitchen, as well as one or two wooden spoons and an unbreakable mixing bowl. The children can pretend to cook with these. Also bring a small tablecloth, plastic plates, cutlery and cups for the children to lay the table. You may be able to talk about families eating together, and about Adam, Eve, Cain and Abel eating food together.

2s - 3s
You can glue a mural of families with 2s and 3s today. Also, bring fruits and vegetables as suggested for babies. Let the children taste peeled pieces of apple and carrot. One or two bites of each is all that children need - it is not a meal!

Make a sequence puzzle Find pictures of a baby, toddler, child, teenager, adult and older person. Make a set of males and a set of females. Mount each picture on a piece of lightweight card. Help the children arrange the pictures according to age. Use the pictures to talk about families and about how God plans for us to grow.

3s - 5s
You can use the fruit and vegetable 'feeling and tasting' activity, as well as the sequence puzzles. You may want to bring cardboard boxes for the children to climb in and out of, but they would need to be fairly large. A local electrical appliance retailer may be willing to let you have a large box. It is probably best to have only one. Two or three boxes could make things rather crowded and may cause the children to become over-excited, which often leads to accidents.

In addition:
Make a puzzle of things we use Collect several everyday items from around the house: a hairbrush or comb, a toothbrush, a spoon, a plastic cup, a large key, a purse, etc. Arrange them on a piece of lightweight card and draw around their outlines. Invite the children to place each item on its matching outline shape. Talk about the everyday things that families use at home.

Make a family booklet for each child Cut A4 sheets of light-coloured paper in quarters. Punch holes along one side of the papers so that they can be made into booklets. Use 30 cm lengths of wool to tie the booklets together. You will need enough pieces of paper in each booklet for the children to have a page for each member of their family. Write, 'God loves my family' on the front cover of each one. Provide crayons for the children to draw each member of their family. They may want to include family members who do not live at their house, or even a pet. Some children will find drawing difficult, so if they just want to 'scribble' on each page, let them do so. Resist the temptation to draw a picture for them, or tell them what colour to use. Using purple for the hair is not a problem to most three and four-year-olds! You can write the name of the family member on each page if it seems appropriate. Some children will produce beautifully drawn pictures, and will spend most of the morning working on them. Others will sit for two minutes and barely draw a line. However long each child is at the art table, make the most of the opportunity to communicate God's love and plan for families. When a child has finished, write his or her name on the booklet, and tie the pages together loosely with a piece of wool.

Dressing-up in the home corner Bring various items of clothing worn by different ages of people for the children to dress up in. These may include a man's dress shirt, a necktie, a hat or cap, a woman's skirt or blouse. Provide a large mirror for the children to look at themselves: use a child-safety mirror if possible. As they dress up, talk about what different family members wear, and what they do. You may be able to tell part of the Bible story.

Group Time

2s - 3s

As the children come to group time, talk about the different activities they have been involved in. You may want to ask specific children about what they did: 'Matthew, I saw you in the home corner this morning. What were you doing?' Or you can address a question more generally: 'I saw Mrs Smith at the table in the corner. She had something for you to taste. Who can tell me about that?' After you have told the story and talked about today's theme, you could show the pictures used for the sequence puzzle to talk about growing, or to talk about the ages of the members of the children's families.

3s - 5s

As you talk about the morning's activities, try to draw out some of the more quiet children. You may start by asking them to tell you about something they did this morning. Or you may want to ask a more 'directive' question: 'Jonathan, I saw you with some fruits and vegetables this morning. What did you taste?'

After you have told the story and had time for talking, praying or singing, you can bring out the items from the 'things we use' puzzle. Spread them out, one by one, on the floor, inviting the children to name them as you do so. Ask the children to close their eyes while you remove one of the items. As they open their eyes, ask them to raise their hand if they know what is missing. It may take a few times before they get the hang of not shouting out when they know the answer. If they get very adept at this, you can remove two items at a time. Continue with this game as parents arrive.

---

you can write your own songs!

Making up songs for under fives is not as difficult as you may think. It's easy to make up a simple tune or, if you prefer, to borrow one from a nursery rhyme. What really matters is the choice of words. They, too, should be simple and straightforward. Here are a few suggestions. Practise them - and then see if you can make up a song to use. Go on - have a try!

To the tune of the first two lines of 'Twinkle, twinkle, little star', sing 'You are special, yes you are; / There is no one else like you.'

Using do, re, mi, sing this tune: do, re, mi, fa, so, so / so, fa, mi, re, do, do.
Now sing these words to it: 'Mary was so happy / She would have a baby boy.'

Here's another tune: so, so, fa, mi, re, do, do / so, so, fa, mi, re, do / do, re, mi, fa, so, so, so / so, so, fa, mi, re do.

Now sing these words to it: 'The angel came to Mary. / He had some news to bring. / You will have a baby boy / And he will be God's son.'

You will also find a good selection of easy-to-sing songs in *100 Action Songs for Preschoolers* and *100 Action Songs for Toddlers* (David C Cook Publishing Company).

Take Home!

THE FIRST FAMILY (GENESIS 1-4)

Aim
To help the children understand that God made families; that families were God's idea.

Bible verses
God looked at everything he made and it was very good. (Genesis 1:31)
God made a man and a woman. (Genesis 1:27)
God cares for you. (1 Peter 5:7)
God planned for families. (Genesis 2:24)

The story
A long time ago God made the first family. God made a man. His name was Adam. Adam lived by himself in the beautiful world God had made. He gave names to all the different kinds of animals. Adam was lonely, though, because he was the only person that God had made.

God did not want Adam to be lonely. So he made a woman. Her name was Eve. Adam loved Eve. They enjoyed all the things that God had made. They ate fruits and vegetables from the trees and plants.

God planned for Adam and Eve to have children. They had a baby boy. His name was Cain. Adam and Eve took care of Cain. After a while they had another baby. His name was Abel. Adam and Eve and their children were the first family.

Activity suggestions
Look at family photo albums
Spend a few minutes with your child this week looking at family photographs. You can even do this with your baby. For a baby, choose photos that show people clearly, without too much clutter. As you hold your baby, tell him / her about who is in the photos. Tell your baby about the first family.

Older under fives will enjoy looking at pictures of themselves as babies. If you have childhood photos of yourself and other adult members of your family they may enjoy these as well. As you enjoy talking about your own family, tell your child about Adam and Eve. Thank God for families.

Special request In two weeks time we shall be continuing the theme of families as we look at the story of Ruth. We should like to look at family photographs with the children and would be pleased if your child could bring one or two family snaps to the session. We shall, of course, return the pictures to you afterwards.

Make a 'gadget' puzzle
Collect several commonly used items from around the house, such as a hairbrush or comb, a toothbrush, a key, a spoon, etc. Arrange them on a large piece of paper or card and draw around them. Let your child match the items to the outlines on the paper. Talk about things families use in the home. Tell your child the Bible verses for this week.

God Gives us Families   Week 2

NOAH'S FAMILY LOVED GOD (GENESIS 6 - 9)

Aim To help the children understand that God wants people to love him; that families can love God.

Preparation

Today's story comes from Genesis 6:9 - 7:16, but for us as teachers it is helpful to read the whole account as indicated above. As you read the story, you may have many questions (join the queue!) and commentaries don't answer all of them. We will probably not know the answers until we see Jesus face to face. So let's focus on one or two of the certainties of this story.

The wickedness of humanity had persisted and increased to such an extent that God determined judgement to be the only answer. His heart was broken because humankind was choosing to go its own way. But into this sad picture comes Noah, a man who walked with God. His life and the lives of his family are saved and, because of Noah's faithfulness to God, the human race was saved from complete destruction. After the flood, Noah and his family represented, and actually were, a new beginning. This makes our teaching aim for today a very significant one. Because of Noah's love for God, the human race was preserved. His family was certainly an important one.

Here is a challenging and encouraging thought for us: God didn't choose Noah because he was perfect. God chose Noah because he desired to be righteous, and he pursued that desire. Because of that, God set him apart for a very high purpose. Take a few minutes to renew your commitment in the words of the song: 'My heart's one desire is to be holy, set apart for you, Lord. I choose to be holy, set apart for you, my Master, ready to do your will.'(Brian Doerkson, Mercy Publishing / Thankyou Music)

As teachers, we should be encouraged by the potential of our lives when given over completely to God. We want to communicate to the children that people love God, and that whole families can love God together. Many of the older under fives will know the story of Noah. That is, they will know about the ark, the animals, the flood and the rainbow. Whether they have any understanding of the story's significance is another matter.

Let's pray that as we teach this week, we will help all the children to understand one of the most important things about this story - that Noah loved God. If that had not been the case, there would have been no story. Arks and animals may make good reading for under fives, but they don't necessarily convey a Biblical truth. Focusing on Noah's love for God, and the fact that God wants us to love him will help to build the foundations of faith in the children's lives.

'Thank you, Lord, that many of the children I teach are part of whole families that love you. For those children whose families are not united by faith, I pray that you will help me to be sensitive as I teach. For the members of my own family who do not yet know you, I pray that your Holy Spirit would be at work in their lives. Amen.'

Story Time

Bible verses
Noah loved God. (Genesis 6:9)
Noah and his family did what God said. (Genesis 7:13)
God wants us to love him. (Exodus 20:3)
God wants us to obey him and do things that please him. (Deuteronomy 6:3)

Birth - 2s Noah loved God. He wanted to do the things that pleased God. Noah had a wife and three sons. One day God told Noah to build an ark. An ark is a very big boat. God wanted it to be big enough to put two of every kind of animal in it. Noah and his family would live in it, too. Noah did just what God told him to do. God was glad that Noah loved him. God took care of Noah and his family.

3s - 5s

Noah was a man who loved God. He wanted to do the things that pleased God. Noah had a wife and three sons. His sons were called Ham, Shem and Japheth. They were married too. One day God told Noah to do something very special. He wanted Noah to build an ark. An ark is a very big boat. God told Noah all about how he wanted him to build it. It was to be big enough to put two of every kind of animal into it. Noah and all his family would live in it too.

Noah did exactly what God told him to do. It took a long time to build the ark. When it was ready, the animals came to Noah. He put them in the ark. Noah and his family went inside the ark.

God was pleased that Noah loved him. He was glad that Noah did what he had asked him to do. God took care of Noah and his family.

Teaching Activities

As we talk to and with children of all ages today, let's be joyful about the fact that we can love God. In keeping with our theme of families, let's be natural about the idea that whole families can love God.

Babies

Observe water in a bottle Fill a few small clear plastic bottles about two-thirds full with water, then add several drops of green or blue food colouring. For older babies, you could use a two-litre bottle. Screw the top on tightly. The babies will be drawn to the sight and sound of water sloshing around in the bottle. Those who are old enough to hold toys will enjoy shaking the bottle themselves. As the babies play with the bottles, tell some of the Bible story.

Water play Fill a plastic washing-up bowl with lukewarm water and place it on a waterproof sheet. Even young babies can splash their hands in the water. Older babies will need to wear plastic aprons for this activity. Because close supervision is necessary, only one or two children can be involved in this activity at any time. As babies splash their hands, thank God for the water, for a drink of water, for a bath. Give thanks to God for hands to splash and play. Such conversation may seem simplistic, but it helps to teach young children that every good thing comes from God, and will help them to be natural in talking to, and about, God.

Make a pull toy Obtain a shallow cardboard box with a base measuring roughly 20 cm by 10 cm. Cover it with coloured paper. Punch a hole in one end of the box. Thread a 50 cm length of string through the hole and knot it on the inside of the box. Tie an empty cotton reel at the other end of the string, so that a baby may grasp it and pull the box along. Even a baby who is only sitting can pull the string to make the box move. Some babies might enjoy putting things such as wooden bricks into the box. As babies play, tell them that God loves them, and that they can love God too. A statement such as, 'God loves you, Rebecca. You can love him too' is sufficient.

Listen to relaxing music Bring a portable cassette player and play a recording of some quiet, relaxing music as 'background' to help set a calm atmosphere in the room. A baby might be near the player, and you can draw his attention to the music: 'Thank you, God, for nice music to listen to. I'm glad God loves us and gives us good things', is a simple yet profound theological statement that will build a child's understanding that all good things come from God (James 1:17).

Toddlers

Even a room full of toddlers can have a relaxed atmosphere. Relaxed teachers are the key, but you may also want to play a tape of music today, as suggested for the babies. Bottles of water will be great fun for toddlers, as will water play, for which the children should wear aprons. You may want to add a few small items to the water so that the children can scoop and pour.

Toddlers may enjoy loading bricks into a pull toy and pulling it around the room. As they work to do this, you may be able to say: 'You are working to put the bricks in the box. Noah and his family worked hard to build the ark, as God told them to. They loved God and wanted to do what he said.'

An additional activity for toddlers is:
Paint with coloured salt Half fill two salt-shakers with salt, then add a teaspoon of dry powder paint. Use a different colour in each shaker. You will also need plain paper, glue, and glue brushes. Let children 'paint' with glue on the paper. When they have finished, give them the shakers to sprinkle over the wet glue. Gently shake any excess coloured salt into the bin and set the pictures aside to dry. Close supervision will be necessary, so only one or two children at a time can participate in this activity. As children take turns with the salt shakers, you can remind them, 'The Bible says, "Do the things that please God." When you take turns so nicely, you are doing what the Bible says.' This may lead naturally into telling a few sentences of the Bible story of Noah and his family who did what pleased God.

2s - 3s

Water play, bottles of coloured water, a pull toy and painting with coloured salt are all appropriate activities for two-to-three years olds. You may find that trying to play quiet background music may actually add to the noise of the room, so you may want to leave that idea.

In addition you can:
Play a verse-matching game Cut seven strips (4 cm by 20 cm) of variously coloured paper. Cut seven squares (10 cm) from the same colours. Look through old magazines or catalogues to find small pictures of a baby, a young boy, a young girl, a teenage boy, a teenage girl, a woman and a man. You will need two of each. As the children will be trying to match them up it is helpful if the pairs are as similar as possible. Glue one set onto the paper strips and the other onto the matching coloured squares.

Print a different Bible verse on each strip, choosing from the verses we are using in this unit. Place the markers into the Bible at the appropriate place, with the pictures showing at the top. Lay the squares out on the floor. A child can choose a square picture, then try to find the matching marker in the Bible. If a child is struggling, it might help to say: 'The picture of the little girl is on red paper. Can you find another picture of a little girl on red paper?' Although most two-year-olds can't name colours correctly, they can usually match them up visually. Help a child as much as is necessary, then open the Bible and read the verse. The interest level and maturity of the child will determine how much you talk about the verse, and whether you can link it to today's story.

3s - 5s

Even this age group will enjoy bottles filled with coloured water. Two two-litre bottles might be best, one blue and one green if you have the right food colouring. Water play is fascinating for children of all ages, so try to include it in today's activities. You may want to add some plastic boats to the water, giving opportunities to talk about Noah's love for, and obedience to, God in building the ark. Painting with coloured salt will be enjoyable for 3s to 5s. The Bible verse-matching game can be used, too. To add interest, you may want to turn the squares face down; the child then chooses a colour and turns it over to see what the picture is.

An additional activity might be:

Hammer nails into wood You can obtain some large blocks of wood from someone in your church who is in the building trade, or by going to a timber merchant who will probably be glad to let you have a few off-cuts if you explain what you want them for. Choose a soft wood and check that it is free of splinters. You will need one or two hammers, and some long nails with large heads. It goes without saying that this activity needs extremely close supervision (one adult per child), and should not even be put out until an adult can stay with it constantly. Most children of this age will be able to manage hammering large nails, even if they need a bit of help. Many of them may not have attempted this before. Alternatively, base this activity on work with a set of 'play' hammer and pegs made from wood or plastic. As the children hammer, you can easily talk with them about Noah building the ark. Remember that our focus is not so much the ark, but Noah's obedience and love for God.

Group Time

2s - 3s

Sing songs to describe today's activities. For example, to the tune of 'Here we go round the mulberry bush' you could sing: 'It's fun to play with water at church, water at church, water at church. It's fun to play with water at church, I like to come to church.' You could substitute different phrases each time, always ending with 'I like to come to church': 'It's fun to paint a picture'; 'I like to look at books'; 'I can read the Bible' and so on. Move into the other elements of group time - Bible story, prayer, conversation - in the order which seems best. The pattern can change from week to week. At the end of group time, as you wait for parents to collect their children, use the verse-matching game, going round the circle to let children take turns. Don't worry if three children in a row choose the same picture. They have not yet worked out that the same picture always results in the same verse being read!

3s - 5s

The ideas and songs suggested for 2s - 3s today can be used with 3s - 5s also. When playing the Bible verse game at the end, you may want to whisper the verse to a child, then let him say it aloud for the others to hear. Some children will respond enthusiastically to this idea, others will not. Let them choose whether you read it or whisper to them. It may also be an idea to remove a square after a child has chosen it to avoid repetition. When all squares are gone, lay them out again to let the rest of the children have a turn.

Take Home!

NOAH'S FAMILY LOVED GOD
(GENESIS 6 - 9)

Aim
To help the children understand that God wants people to love him; that families can love God.

Bible Verses
Noah loved God. (Genesis 6:9)
Noah and his family did what God said. (Genesis 7:13)
God wants us to love him. (Exodus 20:3)
God wants us to obey him and do things that please him. (Deuteronomy 6:3)

The Story
Noah was a man who loved God. He wanted to do the things that pleased God. Noah had a wife and three sons. His sons were called Ham, Shem and Japheth. They were married too. One day God told Noah to do something very special. He wanted Noah to build an ark. An ark is a very big boat. God told Noah all about how he wanted him to build it. It was to be big enough to put two of every kind of animal into it. Noah and all his family would live in it too.

Noah did exactly what God told him to do. It took a long time to build the ark. When it was ready, the animals came to Noah. He put them in the ark. Noah and his family went inside the ark.

God was pleased that Noah loved him. He was glad that Noah did what he had asked him to do. God took care of Noah and his family.

Activity Suggestions
Water play
Most children enjoy water play and may enjoy playing in the bath. Set your child up at the sink or on the floor with water in a washing-up bowl. (If you have a very young baby, you may just want to talk about Noah at bathtime. But even with a small baby, you could splash hands and feet in some warm water other than at bath time.)

For older under fives, investigate sinking and floating with a variety of objects. Or collect some pebbles and wash them in the water. Tell your child about Noah as you enjoy water play together.

Play a Bible verse game
Cut some bookmark-size strips of paper and write a Bible verse on each one. Use today's verses and also those from last week. Place them in your Bible at the correct reference. (Children won't be too bothered about chapter and verse, but seeing the markers in the Bible helps them to understand that these words come from the Bible.)

Let your child choose a marker. Tell him or her what the Bible says. Your child may want to repeat the words after you. If you have a young baby, you can hold him or her on your lap while you open the Bible and say, 'The Bible says...'. As small children hear this repeated over time, it will begin to take on significance for them.

God Gives us Families   Week 3

A HAPPY FAMILY (RUTH)

Aim To help the children learn that God planned for families to love each other; that families look after each other.

Preparation

The story of Naomi, Ruth and Boaz is a wonderful story of love and loyalty.

For our purposes in teaching today, we want to concentrate on Ruth's initial loyalty to Naomi, and on the closing scene of the story where we see Naomi, Boaz, Ruth and the baby Obed as a family together. But for our personal growth as Christians, there are some other aspects of the story we can consider.

Firstly, Ruth's declaration that she will stay with Naomi is not just a case of being a faithful and caring daughter-in-law, although it certainly is that. It also indicates Ruth's 'conversion' to the worship of Yahweh, the one true God. Even in the sadness and grief that fell upon Naomi in Moab (the loss of her husband and two sons), something caused Ruth to want to know the God Naomi worshipped. Maybe it was the fact that Naomi hoped in God in the midst of her affliction that helped Ruth see the reality of a God of grace.

We don't want to read things into the text that aren't there, but it is a good reminder to us that what 'speaks' to non-Christians is not always upbeat, happy, 'praise-the-Lord' personalities. Sometimes it is when they see us as 'real' people, with problems, griefs and disappointments, yet whose faith is strong, that they want to know the God we serve.

The story of the developing relationship between Ruth and Boaz is a beautiful one that combines loyalty to duty with love.

Because Ruth and Naomi were both childless widows, their prospects were dismal. There was no one with any responsibility for them, and no hope of carrying on the family name. Enter Boaz - the 'kinsman redeemer'. An ancient law of Moses said that if a woman was widowed without any sons, the nearest male relative could buy her husband's land, and also sleep with the woman so that she could bear sons who would then carry on her dead husband's family line. This relationship did not necessarily imply marriage.

Although Boaz was a kinsman, he had no obligation to 'redeem' Ruth. In fact, there was a complication of a nearer kinsman, who legally had right of 'first refusal'. Boaz very cleverly managed to get this other kinsman to opt out of the chance of buying the land and getting Ruth in the bargain. His duty was only to enable Ruth to have sons, but he chose to marry her as well. Most scholars would agree that not only was Boaz fulfilling a family duty, he was marrying a woman whom he had grown to love.

This is one story that has a truly happy ending. Boaz and Ruth get each other, and a baby son. Naomi gets a grandson to carry on the family name, and security for her old age. And God's purposes in human history are beautifully worked out, for Ruth and Boaz's son, Obed, is the grandfather of King David, from whom Jesus was descended.

'Thank you, Lord, for the story of Ruth. Thank you for ways my own family cares for me, and for ways my church family cares for me. For any children in my group who come from families that are not committed to loving and looking after one another, I pray they will know some security in my love for them, and a growing understanding of your love for them. Amen.'

Week 3

Story Time

Bible verses
Ruth loved Naomi. (Ruth 4:15)
Naomi helped Ruth look after baby Obed. (Ruth 4:16)

Birth - 2s
Naomi and Ruth lived in Bethlehem. Ruth looked after Naomi. She was part of Naomi's family.

Ruth married a man named Boaz. They loved each other. They had a baby boy. His name was Obed. Naomi was his grandmother. She was happy to have a grandson. She loved him very much. Naomi helped Ruth look after baby Obed. Naomi held baby Obed on her lap, and fed him.

Naomi, Ruth, Boaz and baby Obed were a happy family. They loved each other. They looked after each other.

3s - 5s
Naomi and Ruth lived together in Bethlehem. Ruth was part of Naomi's family. She had promised to stay with Naomi and look after her.

Ruth went to the fields to pick up pieces of grain. She and Naomi could use the grain to make bread. The field belonged to a kind man named Boaz. After a while Ruth married Boaz. They loved each other.

Ruth and Boaz had a baby boy. His name was Obed. Naomi was his grandmother. She was happy to have a grandson and she loved him very much. She helped Ruth look after baby Obed. Naomi held him on her lap and fed him.

Naomi, Ruth, Boaz and baby Obed were a happy family. They loved each other. They looked after each other.

Teaching Activities

It is very difficult to find one verse that summarizes the Bible's teaching on family life. Although we cannot show specific words in the Bible to the children, we are certainly being true to the Word when we tell them that the Bible says that God planned for families to love and look after one another. We must be sensitive to those children whose families do not love and look after each other. But we still want to be clear about God's perfect plan for families.

Babies
Make a board book about family members Cut out pictures of babies, children, teenagers, mums, dads and grandparents from magazines. Glue them onto some cardboard. Use both sides. On one card write 'God loves families'; this can be the cover of the book. Punch two holes on the left-hand side of each card and tie them together with wool or ribbon. Although many books about families are available in the shops, even babies will like the simplicity of a home-made one. To make the book more durable, cover the pages with clear, sticky-backed plastic. You can also use the book you made in Week 1. As you show the pictures to a baby, you can say thank you to God for the members of that baby's family. The words 'mummy' or 'daddy' will be familiar even to a very young baby.

Look at a goldfish Bring a goldfish in a clear plastic container with a secure lid. It is likely that there will be someone in the church who is willing to let his or her fish visit the children for a couple of hours. As a baby lies on the floor, place the goldfish in front of him or her. Sing to the baby about the goldfish swimming in the water. Thank God for eyes to see the fish, or for the fish itself. Leave the lid off the container until the session starts, then remove it after the session. If the container is only about three-quarters full of water, there will be plenty of oxygen to last the session.

Water paint a cardboard box Bring a large cardboard box for older babies. Cover the floor with a waterproof sheet and a few layers of newspaper. Provide spill-proof paint pots half full of water, chunky children's paintbrushes and some form of painting apron. Let babies 'paint' the box. You may need to dip the paint brush for them, and show them how to stroke it against the box. This activity lets older babies have the experience of painting, but without the mess. The worst that can happen is that they get wet - but it is only water! You will need to watch that they don't put paint-brushes in their mouths. One or two babies painting at one time is probably the most you can manage. As the babies enjoy what is probably a new experience, talk to them about their family, or tell a sentence or two of the Bible story.

Toddlers

Toddlers will enjoy looking at a board book of family members, and watching a goldfish. You may want to feed the fish while they watch. Water painting a box will be fun, but you could also use real paint if you have enough adult supervision. It might help to limit the mess of real paint if you place the box on a very low table. Children seem to make less mess if they can stand up - at least it keeps their legs and shoes out of the way!

In addition you could:
Care for a doll Although you may normally provide a doll in the home corner, you could bring extra items for the doll today. Perhaps a change of clothes, a nappy (you can make one from a square of white cloth if you haven't got access to newborn-sized disposables), a towel for pretend bathing. A bottle, a baby bowl and a spoon would add interest. If you have the space you might even want to provide a small doll's pram or buggy, although this will mean an adult has to help the children take turns! As the children help to care for the doll, tell parts of the Bible story. Talk about how Naomi and Ruth must have cared for Obed. Talk about those toddlers who have babies at home.

2s - 3s

Two and three-year-olds will enjoy watching a goldfish, and may want to help you feed it. You may want to bring the same items for the doll as suggested for toddlers. Rather than pretending to bath the doll, you can provide a plastic bowl full of warm soapy water for real washing. Place the bowl on a low table covered with newspaper, and put plastic aprons on the children. You may need two or three towels for the doll as it will probably get washed several times! Remember that water play requires close supervision at all times.

In addition:
Paint at the easel Cover the floor and provide painting aprons for the children. Provide two different colours of paint and large sheets of paper. Many children of this age tend to put all the paint in one place on their paper. This is fine, but you may need to tell them that their painting won't dry quickly if they put all the paint in one place. For those children who would paint all day if you let them, you may need to say: 'You may dip your brush two more times, then you will need to finish so someone else can have a turn.' Sing to the children while they paint: 'I like to paint at church' or 'It's fun to paint at the easel' are appropriate words. You may also have opportunities to tell a bit of the Bible story to children as they paint.

Make a photo album If the requests made in the preceding two weeks have worked you should have an adequate supply of family photographs. Bring an empty photo album and let the children help you put the photos into it. Include one or two pictures of the adults, perhaps as young children or with their present families. Children love to look at pictures of themselves and of one another. This activity provides many natural opportunities for exploring the themes of this unit.

3s - 5s

Looking at the goldfish, easel painting and bathing the doll are all suitable activities for today. Making a photo album of the children's pictures should also prove to be very enjoyable.

You may also want to:

Provide stand-up family figures in the brick area From a magazine cut out full-length pictures of a baby, one or two children, a mother, a father, and one or two older adults if possible. Glue them on thin card then cut around them. Glue each figure to an empty cardboard roll so that they will stand up. Put these with the bricks. The children may want to build houses for them, or just look at them. As you talk about the figures, you can also talk about God's plan for family members to care for one another.

Have a visit from a mother and baby Ask a mother (and father, if possible) with a fairly young baby to visit the children. They could show the children how they look after their baby. If they could arrange the timing right, they could give the baby a bottle. (Many children would be quite used to seeing a baby breast fed, but for those who haven't seen this, it may provoke questions that are not easy to deal with in the context of the class. It may well be best to stick with a baby that will take a bottle!) Such a visit will lead to easy conversation about how Naomi and Ruth looked after the baby Obed.

Group Time

2s - 3s

To signal that it is time to tidy the room and get ready for group time, try singing (to the tune of 'Here we go round the mulberry bush'): 'It's time to put the toys away ... and you can be a helper.' Some children will quickly join in putting things away. Other children need to be encouraged by being given a specific task.

You may want to start group time by looking at the goldfish. When you are ready to tell the Bible story, place the fish where it won't be a distraction to the children.

After telling the story, ask the children if they would like to say a thank-you prayer to God for their families. Don't worry if none of them want to. Just say a simple prayer yourself, thanking God for Naomi and her family, and for our families who love us and take care of us.

You can finish by looking again at the photo album of the children's pictures. If you can't slide the photos out as each parent arrives, keep them until next week. Very few parents will need the pictures back immediately!

3s - 5s

If the visiting parent and baby have stayed through all of activity time, they will need to leave now so the children can concentrate on clearing up and on group time. All the suggestions made for the 2s and 3s will work here as well. In addition to looking again at the photo album, you might want to finish with a guessing game involving everyday family activities. You could mime various activities and let the children guess what you are doing: for example, combing hair, cleaning teeth, getting dressed, having a bath.

3s - 5s

You can use the songs about church while children are playing and working. Children of this age will also enjoy the Bible marker and beanbag activity.

Build a 'town' with the bricks Place a variety of small boxes with the bricks to be made into houses, shops, churches, etc. You may also want to provide some twigs and leaves to make trees; stand them up in playdough or modelling clay. You could add some cars, and mark out roads with masking tape if you want. This activity will provide good opportunities for conversations about a range of things related to today's theme.

Paint with cars Cover the floor and work surface. The children should wear aprons for this activity. Put a small amount of paint into a shallow pan or dish. Place one or two cars in the pan, including one or two with patterned tyre tread if possible. Give the children a fairly large sheet of paper and let them run the car wheels over their paper to make any pattern they wish. Use two colours of paint if you want, although you will have to watch that the cars stay in the right colour. Painting with cars will lead to conversations about how the children travel to church, and about how Jesus went to church.

Play musical instruments If your church does not have a set of children's musical instruments, you may be able to borrow some from a school or play group. Place them in a corner of the room. The children may just want to play them, or play as you sing the songs about the church. Very few children of this age can play and sing at the same time! You may limit this activity to one or two short periods during the teaching time in order not to wear out the teachers' ears!

Group Time

2s - 3s

Use the songs about church as children come to group time. Bring the stones and shells, and pick out one or two of the most unusual ones to hold up for the children. Talk about their shapes, colours and textures. After telling the Bible story ask if any of the children want to say thank you to God for something we do at church. Don't force a child to pray, but try to provide the opportunity for those who are willing. Ask a child what he or she enjoyed doing this morning, then suggest they say thank you to God for that thing. It is not necessary for children to bow heads and close their eyes to pray. Some may be accustomed to doing this, some may not. It is important that we help children learn to be quiet while others are praying or talking: this is simply common courtesy.

While you are waiting for parents to collect their children, bring out the Bible marker activity and let the children take turns throwing the beanbag and hearing verses read.

3s - 5s

As the children come to group time let each one have a musical instrument. If there are not enough to go round, they can take turns and children without instruments can clap their hands. Let them follow a teacher around the room as they play and sing (to the tune of 'Here we go round the mulberry bush'):

It's fun to march around the room, around the room, around the room,
It's fun to march around the room, around the room with our friends.

As with the 2s and 3s, give children the opportunity to pray after you tell the story. Use the Bible marker activity as parents arrive to collect their children.

Take Home!

JESUS' FAMILY WENT TO CHURCH (LUKE 2:41-52)

Aim
To help each child learn that Jesus' family went to church; that families can go to church together.

Bible Verses
Jesus went to church with his family. (Luke 2:42)
Jesus talked to the teachers at church. (Luke 2:46)
Jesus went to church. (Luke 4:16)

The Story
Jesus and his family were going to church. They went every week to the church in their village. But this was a special trip. They were going to the big church in Jerusalem. It was called the Temple. They did not have cars or trains to take them to Jerusalem. They would walk, or ride on a donkey. It would take them a few days to get there.

When they got to Jerusalem, Jesus went to the Temple. He wanted to ask the teachers many questions. They wanted to talk to him as well. He was busy learning about God when his family left. Mary and Joseph had to go back and look for him.

They found him at the Temple. He said to them, 'Didn't you know that I wanted to stay here to learn more about God? I like to be here at church.' Then they went home together. Perhaps on the way home they talked about some of the things Jesus had learned at the Temple.

Activity Suggestions
Look at a book with pictures of churches
This may necessitate a trip to the library to find a book with pictures of various churches and cathedrals. Look at it with your child. Talk about what church might have been like when Jesus went. Tell your child about Jesus going to church.

For a young baby, talk about your own church and the different things that happen there. Tell your baby about Jesus going to church.

Make a collage of different forms of transport
Look in old magazines for pictures of cars, buses, trains, and even horses and carts. If your child can manage scissors, let him or her cut out the pictures and glue them onto paper. As you work together, talk about the different ways that people travel to your church. Talk about Jesus going to church with Mary and Joseph.

God Gives us Families   Week 5

AQUILA AND PRISCILLA (ACTS 18:1-4, 18-26)

Aim To help children understand that families work together and help each other; that families can tell others about Jesus.

Preparation

Like so many biblical characters Aquila and Priscilla receive only a brief mention, yet the ripple of their influence spread wide. When Paul came to Corinth he needed two things: friends and employment. Paul was a rabbi, and the tradition was that all rabbis learned a trade so that they could support themselves. Paul's trade was tent making, as was Aquila and Priscilla's. These three not only worked together to make a living, but they shared a home for a time as well. Later, Aquila and Priscilla accompanied Paul as he started his next missionary journey.

Enter Apollos, a learned man and a brilliant preacher. He had heard about Jesus, and was preaching what he knew. But he didn't know of the baptism that Jesus demonstrated - the move from the old life to the new, and the empowering of the Holy Spirit for this new life. Aquila and Priscilla were mature, sensitive folk. Instead of correcting him publicly, they took him on one side and 'more accurately explained the way of God to him' (Acts 18:26).

This brief story challenges us about how we treat adults and help them to maturity. It also encourages us to see the potential in the children we work with, and to be sensitive in how we correct them. Who knows what they will grow up to be and do in the kingdom of God? How encouraging to think that we play a part in building the foundations of their lives!

This story helps us communicate today's theme. Aquila and Priscilla were a family, and for a time Paul became part of that family. They all worked together in business. In that context, they helped each other. But it must have been more than that. Paul had been through some rough times in his ministry, and when he came to Corinth he needed encouragement. He surely looked to his 'family' there for emotional and spiritual support as well as food and lodging. They all worked together and helped each other in daily life and for the sake of the gospel.

As we teach, let's ask God to help us capture a joyful vision of families working together and helping each other, not only in the practical things of life, but also in the work of the kingdom. As this is the last week of this unit, let's pray that the children will have absorbed positive and godly input about families through our teaching and activities.

'Heavenly Father, as I think about families working together, thank you that you don't ask us to be perfect - only available. Please help me to be very available to you in my teaching this week. Help me to communicate the fullness of life with you through words, actions and attitudes. For the glory of your name I pray, Amen.'

Story Time

Bible verses
Aquila and Priscilla worked together. (Acts 18:3)
Aquila and Priscilla helped a man learn more about Jesus. (Acts 18:26)
We work together. (2 Corinthians 1:24)

Birth - 2s
Aquila and Priscilla worked together. They made tents for people to live in. One day Paul came to their city. He made tents too. Paul and Aquila and Priscilla worked together. They lived in the same house, like a family.

Paul, Aquila and Priscilla loved Jesus. They liked to talk to people about Jesus. They helped people to know more about him.

Paul and Aquila and Priscilla helped each other as they worked together making tents. They helped each other at church, too, when they told people about Jesus.

3s - 5s

Aquila and Priscilla were married. They worked together. They made tents for people to live in. One day a man named Paul came to their city. He made tents too. He wanted to work and find a place to live.

Aquila and Priscilla let Paul work with them. They all made tents together. Paul lived in their house with them. He was like part of their family.

Paul, Aquila and Priscilla loved Jesus. They liked to talk to people about Jesus. They helped people to know more about him.

Paul and Aquila and Priscilla lived together as a family. They helped each other as they worked to make tents. They helped each other at church, too, when they told people more about Jesus.

Teaching Activities

As the children do things together this morning, and as we do things with them, we can talk about Paul, Aquila and Priscilla working together, going to church together and telling people about Jesus together. I am sure that God intended that all these activities should be natural ones for families. We must not be critical of those families where they are not (perhaps even our own?), but should remember that we are teaching God's plan, though we often fall short of it.

Babies

Use books and pictures from previous sessions You may already have been doing this. As this is the last week of this unit, bring out all the books and pictures you have made or used. Even if you have been using them every week, the babies will not be tired of them. They learn by repetition. Seeing them once a week for five weeks is not overdoing it!

Listen to an instrumental recording You may want to use the same one you used a few weeks ago. Listening to a favourite, relaxing tape of your own will help set the tone for you, and thus benefit the babies as well!

Make a 'fill and dump' toy You could use a large plastic sweet jar (these are easily obtainable from shops that sell loose sweets) or some other type of plastic container. Any number of different items are suitable for filling and dumping: stickle bricks, coloured cotton reels, pegs, sponges cut into hand-sized pieces, old plastic hair curlers or plastic lids from various bottles and jars (make sure they are not small enough to be swallowed). Choose just one item this time. Older babies will enjoy putting the items in the jar, then dumping them out and doing it all over again. 'Thank you, God, for hands to play with the toys', is a simple, but important teaching statement. As babies play, you can also tell them the Bible verses for today, or part of the story.

Finger-paint with baby lotion This is an activity for the adventurous! Bring a wipe-clean tray or non-stick baking tray and some baby lotion. Place a small amount of lotion onto the tray, and help an older baby to rub his finger (or fingers) around in the lotion. Some may be very uncertain about this, others will love it. To ensure that lotion-covered fingers don't go into mouths, this should be a 'one adult to one baby' activity. When they have finished, all you have to do is wipe their hands with a tissue. Talk to babies about how the lotion feels on their hands. Thank God for hands to feel.

Toddlers

All of the activities suggested for babies today are entirely appropriate for toddlers.

In addition, you may want to:

Make a tent to play in Bring a large blanket. Place it over a table to make a tent. You may want to bring a sleeping bag to put in the tent, or just place the table on a bit of carpet so the children aren't sitting on a cold floor. You could put some of the books or pictures in the tent, and an adult may even want to go in the tent to look at them with the children. The presence of an adult in the tent will help some children to feel more secure about going in. Resist the temptation to use a ready-made 'Wendy house'. Part of the purpose of this activity is the development of imagination. Obviously, this activity will lead to conversations about the story of Paul, Aquila and Priscilla.

2s - 3s

As with the babies and toddlers, bring any books or pictures you have used in this unit. As children look at them, you can remind them of some of the other stories as well as telling today's story. Making a tent should also be something the children will enjoy. If it is fairly dark inside the tent, you can bring one or two battery-powered torches. Children love torches, but will need to be super-vised so that they are not left switched on for the entire session.

For other activities today, you can:

Make 'food' from playdough Add playdough to the items in the home corner for this session. Assign one teacher to stay in that area to talk and work with the children. They can roll dough to make sausages or chips, or even roll small balls to make peas. It is best to give only a little guidance and let the children make their own food. If an adult makes a masterpiece which the children know they can't match, they will not try to make anything. As they stir dough in a saucepan, or put the 'food' on plates, talk about families working together. Tell part of the Bible story. You might want to talk about Aquila and Priscilla inviting people to their home to learn more about Jesus. Perhaps they prepared food for their visitors.

Make a matching puzzle Obtain two identical brochures from a car showroom. Cut out seven or eight matching sets of pictures, trying to get a mix of colours and styles of cars. Glue one set of pictures on a large piece of paper or card. Place the other pictures next to them, and let the children place a loose picture on its matching pair. When they have all been matched up, shake them off and let another child take a turn. Two or three children may want to work together to match up the pictures. As they take turns, you can say, 'The Bible says, "We work together." You are doing what the Bible says as we work together on this puzzle.' You may then be able to tell part of the Bible story.

Make texture rubbings Provide thin white paper and chunky wax crayons. Look for two or three small items with textured surfaces such as sandpaper, coins, paper clips and the plastic netting used for fruit packaging. Glue each item onto a piece of card. This stops them slipping around when the children colour. You may need to show some children how to colour using the side of the crayon. Even then, they may prefer to hold the crayon in the normal way.

As the children colour, you may be able to talk with them about today's theme. Remember that some children have to concentrate hard on colouring, and silence may be the most effective teacher. A loving adult close by, giving a child time and space to develop his or her own picture is also part of the teaching process. It's not only what we say, it's also what we communicate by our presence and our attitude that teaches the things of God.

3s - 5s

Apart from using books from previous weeks, and making a tent, the suggestions for 3s - 5s today are different. They include:

Sewing in the home corner Cut pieces of lightweight card into the shape of a tent. Punch holes (about 1.5 cm apart) around the edge of each shape. Cut lengths of wool long enough to 'sew' round each tent. Seal the ends by either wrapping them with tape, or dipping them in nail varnish. (You can also use shoe laces.) As children come to the home corner, they can 'sew' a tent shape. Some children will struggle to make the wool go in and out of the holes, others will find it easy. As you work to sew tents, you can talk about Paul, Aquila and Priscilla, and how they worked together to make tents, and to tell people about Jesus.

Observe shells and stones This activity was suggested for 2s - 3s last week. You can use the same rocks and shells. Provide water and towels, as suggested.

'Finger-paint' with shaving foam Bring one or two wipe-clean trays or non-stick baking trays and some shaving foam. Use aprons to cover clothing. Squirt a blob of shaving foam onto the tray, and let children 'finger-paint'. Some of the more enthusiastic children will soon need another blob, others will only venture the tip of one finger to make a pattern. As each new child comes to this activity, give them a fresh blob of foam. Provide a basin of water and a towel for washing hands. (You can add to the impact of this activity by using scented shaving foam.)

Group Time

2s - 3s

Play a game to call the children to group time today. After they have finished helping to put things away, ask them all to stand in one part of the room. Call them one at a time by describing what they are wearing: 'I see a boy wearing blue trousers, who has a teddy on his pullover.' Some of the younger children may not be able to recognize your description of them, but the older ones can help. The children usually enjoy looking around to see who the teacher is describing. As each child is described, they come and sit in the circle. Once they are all seated, a few movement rhymes or songs will probably help to settle them.

After you have told today's story, and given opportunity for conversation and / or prayer, you may want to talk with the children about some of the other stories in this unit. Most of them will not remember them. But if you have their attention, they might like to hear the basics of some of the other stories and their related themes. If the children are a bit restless, the time is better spent in singing or movement. When we are constantly having to remind children to be quiet or sit still, it is best just to move on to something else. While waiting for parents to arrive, give each child a small piece of playdough to roll, pat or squeeze.

3s - 5s

The group time suggestions for 2s and 3s will work for older children as well. These children may remember more details of the stories from past weeks. You may also want to use a recording of household sounds. Record several familiar everyday sounds, such as a doorbell, the telephone, a lavatory flushing, a tap running, a dog barking, a cat purring, a car being started and a vacuum cleaner working. Ask the children to guess the source of each sound. As you thank God for ears to hear these sounds, thank him, too, for ears to hear about Jesus.

Take Home!

AQUILA AND PRISCILLA
(ACTS 18:1-4, 18-26)

Aim
To help children understand that families work together and help each other; that families can tell others about Jesus.

Bible verses
Aquila and Priscilla worked together. (Acts 18:3)
Aquila and Priscilla helped a man learn more about Jesus. (Acts 18:26)
We work together. (2 Corinthians 1:24)

The story
Aquila and Priscilla were married. They worked together. They made tents for people to live in. One day a man named Paul came to their city. He made tents too. He wanted to work and find a place to live.

Aquila and Priscilla let Paul work with them. They all made tents together. Paul lived in their house with them. He was like part of their family.

Paul, Aquila and Priscilla loved Jesus. They liked to talk to people about Jesus. They helped people to know more about him.

Paul and Aquila and Priscilla lived together as a family. They helped each other as they worked to make tents. They helped each other at church, too, when they told people more about Jesus.

Activity suggestions
Make a 'fill-and-dump' toy
This may sound a funny name for a toy but that is exactly what children do with it - they fill it, then dump it! Use a large plastic sweet jar (these are easily obtainable from shops that sell loose sweets) or some other type of plastic container. Any number of different items are suitable for filling and dumping - pegs, sponges cut into hand-sized pieces, old plastic hair curlers or plastic lids from various bottles and jars (make sure they are not small enough to be swallowed). Older babies will enjoy putting the items in the jar, then dumping them out and doing it all over again. Older under fives will enjoy counting the items in and counting them out again. As you play with your child, tell the story of Paul and his friends.

Make a tent to play in
Even if you have a play tent at home, make one 'from scratch' for a change. Drape a large blanket or sheet over a table. Put a sleeping bag, blanket or pillow inside. If it is relatively dark in the 'tent', take a torch inside. Most children are fascinated by torches. As you play in the tent, you can talk about Paul, Aquila and Priscilla making tents. Tell your child the story.

Here Comes Christmas! week 1

MARY HEARS GOOD NEWS (LUKE 1:26-56)

Aim To help the children learn that Jesus' birth was part of God's plan; that Mary was happy about having a special baby.

Preparation

As we look at the story for today, let's try to understand its context. As far as we know, there was nothing unusual about Mary. At the time of her betrothal to Joseph she was probably a teenager.

In those days angelic visitations were not an everyday occurrence. What must Mary have thought when the angel Gabriel came to her with such an unusual message? We don't know what he looked like, or how he came, but something about him made her sure of who he was and the truth of his story.

Mary was obviously a practical girl. Gabriel had given her a message of enormous theological weight. Her response was, 'How can I have a baby? I have never had sex with Joseph, or anyone else.' She wasn't questioning the fact that she would give birth to the 'Son of the Most High' - she was simply wondering how it would happen!

We are left to fill in the details of the story for ourselves: how Mary must have felt, what and when she told her parents and Joseph, and how other people responded when it became obvious that she was pregnant. The human implications of this story are overwhelming. Although Mary was to have an incredible privilege, it had very real and painful consequences. And what was her response? 'Whatever God says, I will do.' Please God, teach us to have that kind of faith and obedience.

So Mary went to visit her relative Elizabeth. The conversation recorded in Luke 1 gives us an idea that Mary and Elizabeth were two women whose lives had been profoundly touched by the Holy Spirit. What must they have talked about in those months they spent together? I wonder if they, like most people, were one day thrilled at what God was doing in their lives and another day terrified? Did they have days when they doubted that they had heard God right? I think they probably did. The Bible isn't about 'super heroes', it is about ordinary people through whom God does extraordinary things. What an encouragement to us!

Mary's song of praise (Luke 1:46-55), known as the Magnificat, must have been sung on a day when she was sure of what God was doing, and aware of the privilege of being part of his plan. It is a beautiful hymn of worship and thanksgiving which has been sung in various forms through the ages. Read it again and try to imagine Mary's wonder at God's greatness and faithfulness. Why not sing or speak your own song of praise to God for his grace and faithfulness in your life?

The practical details of the story will be largely unimportant to the children. Because they don't know about conception, betrothal and shame, the outworkings of this story will escape them. That's fine. They can think about them when they are older. For now, let's communicate the certainty of God's word to Mary and her joyful response. Let's help the children understand that Jesus was part of God's plan and that Mary was happy to be part of that plan as well.

'As we move towards another Christmas, please help me to learn something fresh from you, Lord. As I think about the angel's message to Mary, and her unconditional obedience I am challenged. Please help me to follow your leading as willingly as she did. Amen.'

Story Time

Bible verses

The angel told Mary that God loved her. (Luke 1:28)

Mary was glad that she was going to have a baby named Jesus. (Luke 1:47)

Birth - 2s

Mary loved God. She wanted to do things that made God happy. One day an angel came to tell Mary some news. 'You will have a baby boy,' said the angel. 'His name will be Jesus. He will be God's son.'

Mary said, 'I want to do whatever God wants me to do.'

Mary went to visit her cousin Elizabeth. They were glad to see each other. Mary said, 'I am happy that God has told me about this special baby. I know that God loves me. God always does what he says he will do.'

After Mary had stayed with Elizabeth for three months, she went back to her own home.

3s - 5s

Mary was a young woman who loved God. She wanted to do things that made God happy. One day an angel came to tell Mary some news. An angel brings a message from God. The angel said, 'God loves you. He has some special news for you.' Mary was not sure what the angel meant. 'Don't be afraid,' he said. 'God loves you very much. You will have a baby boy. His name will be Jesus. He will be God's son.'

Mary said, 'I want to do whatever God wants me to do.'

Mary decided to visit her cousin Elizabeth. She was going to have a baby as well. Mary and Elizabeth were glad to see each other. Mary said, 'I am happy that God has told me about this special baby. I know that God loves me. God always does what he says he will do.'

After Mary had stayed with Elizabeth for three months, she went back to her own home.

Teaching Activities

As we begin this unit on Christmas, let's ask God to help us rediscover the thrilling nature of the Christmas story, and forget for a few moments all the busyness in our own lives at this time of year.

Babies

Let babies look in a mirror A hand-held mirror is appropriate for younger babies. Hold it so they can see their face. At this stage of development, they won't know that the face they see is their own. Older babies who are sitting may be able to hold a mirror themselves, so make sure it is one they can easily grasp. They may recognize their own face, or the face of the teacher in the mirror. As a baby looks at himself, say something like: 'Richard, you are special. Jesus was a special baby. Mary was glad to know that she would have a special baby.' Remember not to let babies handle a mirror without supervision. (We recommend that you use unbreakable 'safety mirrors' for this activity.)

Sing songs Make up simple tunes, or use a well-known tune for words such as, 'You are special, there's no one else like you', or, 'Mary was happy, Mary was happy she would have a baby boy'. Any simple words that convey the teaching theme for today are appropriate as are those that help each child to appreciate his or her uniqueness.

Look at nature items Bring items like pine cones, holly leaves and berries for the babies to look at. Put berries and leaves in a transparent document wallet so the babies can't put them in their mouths. Pine cones may be handled if you can supervise closely. Alternatively, put one or two in a clear plastic jar so the babies can see them. As babies look at the nature items you can tell part of the story, or use a Bible verse.

Make a mobile Use a coat hanger to make a mobile for babies to look at. Cut out three or four circles of card (diameter 10 cm). Cut out pictures of babies from old magazines and catalogues. Glue a picture on both sides of each circle and cover with transparent sticky-backed plastic to make them more durable. Punch a hole in each circle and attach them to the hanger with wool, string or very narrow elastic. For older babies you may have to be fairly creative about hanging the mobile in a safe place! As babies look at the pictures you can talk about how they are special and about how Jesus was a special baby.

Toddlers

Toddlers will enjoy the songs suggested for babies. Bring the nature items, too, using the same cautions about berries and prickly leaves. Toddlers will enjoy seeing a head-and-shoulders view of themselves in a large safety mirror. Bring a variety of hats, scarves and gloves for the children to try on as they look at themselves.

In addition:
Make a nature collage Bring lightweight nature items such as leaves, twigs, non-poisonous berries, or even petals of flowers if there are any left. (Remind the children that berries can be dangerous.) Gluing nature items can often prove difficult, so here is a different idea to try. Obtain some dinner-sized paper plates. Cut out the inner circle of each plate, leaving the ribbed edge as a 'frame'. Cut a circle of sticky-backed plastic large enough to cover the hole and stick it to the back of the plate. All the children need to do to make their collage is stick items onto the sticky side of the plastic which is showing through the hole in the plate. As the children work on their collages you can tell part of the Bible story. You could also place the Bible open on the table near where they are working. You could write the Bible verses on a piece of card and lay it on the page. As the children choose nature items to stick you can tell them what the Bible says.

2s - 3s

All of the activities suggested for toddlers will be suitable for two and three-year-olds: songs; nature items; hats, scarves and gloves with a mirror; a nature collage. Because the children are slightly older, you can spread the nature items out on a tray or cloth for them to look at and touch. Let them touch the holly leaves, warning them about the prickles, and supervising them closely.

Other activities you can use include:
Follow the footprints around the room Using brightly coloured paper, cut out several footprint shapes - a tracing of a shoe outline is fine. Stick the footprints to the floor with masking tape or Blutak. Make sure that you space them closely enough so that the children can step from one to the next. Make a path of footprints for them to follow around the room. As children enjoy stepping along the footprint path you can tell part of the story, or talk about Mary going to visit Elizabeth.

Match pairs of 'mittens' Cut out mitten shapes from several different colours of paper. Cut two of each colour so the children can match pairs. Spread them all out and let the children match them up; or put out one mitten from each pair and let the children take the remaining mittens from you one at a time to complete the pairs. You may want to talk about the clothing we wear in winter to keep us warm. It may be appropriate to say, 'Thank you, God for warm clothes to wear.' (Beware of assuming that it was cold in Palestine when Jesus was born. We don't actually know what the exact date of Jesus' birth was - it is possible that the weather was warm!)

3s - 5s

Looking in the mirror while trying on hats, scarves and gloves will be fun for 3s - 5s today. Also, make up some songs, use the mitten-matching game and bring nature items for the children to look at. Although the children will need to be very careful when touching holly, they will probably be interested in the contrast between the smooth surface of the leaves and their prickly edges.

Some other ideas:
Make texture rubbings with nature items Bring some additional nature items for the children to make rubbings: leaves, bits of tree bark, a cutting from an evergreen and small twigs. Provide thin paper, and chunky crayons in autumnal colours.

This activity has value in encouraging talk about things God has made, but you may also be able to tell part of the Bible story as you chat with the children while they work. Don't be afraid of sitting in silence with some children as they colour. Sometimes conversation is not appropriate. We mustn't fall into the trap of thinking that if we aren't talking, we aren't teaching!

Make a mural of baby items Provide a large sheet of paper for making a mural. Place it on the floor, or attach it to the wall at a low level so that an adult can sit to work at it while the children kneel or stand. Obtain a catalogue from a shop that sells baby clothing and equipment, or tear out the appropriate pages from an ordinary mail-order catalogue. Provide scissors and let the children cut out their own pictures of babies and baby items to glue on the mural. Remember, precision cutting isn't the issue here - let each child cut as much as they are able. Only assist if they are struggling. As you work together you can talk about Mary preparing for baby Jesus, or about their baby brothers and sisters at home.

Group Time

2s - 3s

You may want to leave the footprint trail on the floor so that you can lead the children along it as they come to the circle. Use the songs that you have been singing during the session and tell the Bible story. Either say a prayer yourself or ask if any of the children want to say a prayer thanking God for Mary and the news about her special baby. As you wait for parents to come you can play the mitten-matching game as a group. Hand out all the mittens and let the children find the person who has the matching colour. Alternatively, lay one set of colours on the floor, then let the children take turns looking at the top mitten from the pile in your hand and finding the matching colour.

3s - 5s

You may want to start group time by looking at the mural the children have made. Sing a few songs or do one or two finger plays to settle the children, then tell the Bible story. After you have finished you may want to sing the songs you have been using during the session. Pray, giving the children opportunity to say their own prayers if they want to. As you wait for parents you can bring out the tray of nature items again for the children to look at and talk about. Let them tell you if they have been on any walks and seen pine cones, or if they have some of these items in their gardens.

Take Home!

MARY HEARS GOOD NEWS
(LUKE 1:26-56)

Aim
To help the children learn that Jesus' birth was part of God's plan; that Mary was happy about having a special baby.

Bible Verses
The angel told Mary that God loved her. (Luke 1:28)
Mary was glad that she was going to have a baby named Jesus. (Luke 1:47)

The Story
Mary was a young woman who loved God. She wanted to do things that made God happy. One day an angel came to tell Mary some news. An angel brings a message from God. The angel said, 'God loves you. He has some special news for you.' Mary was not sure what the angel meant. 'Don't be afraid,' he said. 'God loves you very much. You will have a baby boy. His name will be Jesus. He will be God's son.'

Mary said, 'I want to do whatever God wants me to do.'

Mary decided to visit her cousin Elizabeth. She was going to have a baby as well. Mary and Elizabeth were glad to see each other. Mary said, 'I am happy that God has told me about this special baby. I know that God loves me. God always does what he says he will do.'

After Mary had stayed with Elizabeth for three months, she went back to her own home.

Activity Suggestions
Make a mobile Use a coat hanger to make a mobile for your baby. Cut out three or four circles of card (diameter 10 cm). Cut out pictures of babies from old magazines and catalogues. Glue a picture on both sides of each circle. Punch a hole in each circle and attach them to the hanger with wool, string or very narrow elastic. As your child looks at the pictures, you can talk about how special he or she is and about how Jesus was a special baby.

Make a baby collage With toddlers and older under fives, work together to make a collage. You will need an old catalogue that contains pictures of babies and baby items. Cut out the pictures for your child to glue. If your child can manage scissors, let him or her do some of the cutting.

As you glue the pictures to make a collage, tell your child about how you prepared for his or her birth. Talk about Mary hearing good news from the angel.

Here Comes Christmas! week 2

JESUS IS BORN (LUKE 2:1-7)

Aim For each child to hear an accurate account of Jesus' birth; to help the children understand that Jesus is special.

Preparation

Joseph had to go to Bethlehem. Mary's baby was due very soon. Why did he take Mary with him? In those days, fathers weren't actively involved in the birth itself. That was left to the women of the family. Perhaps he did not want to leave her to give birth surrounded by gossip and questions of the baby's paternity. Or had he taken in enough of what the angel told him to realize that they had to be in Bethlehem for the birth? Joseph would have known the prophecies. What must he have thought when the news came through about the census, and of the necessity of travelling to Bethlehem?

Bethlehem is about eighty miles from Nazareth. Mary may have walked. Or perhaps they managed to find a donkey for her to ride. Either way, it was hardly a fun-filled romantic honeymoon for a young couple. Accommodation for travellers was very basic. The inns consisted of a series of stalls opening off a common courtyard. The innkeeper provided one central fire for warmth and cooking, and fodder for the animals. The travellers had to bring everything else they needed. Because of Mary's advanced state of pregnancy, the journey would have taken several days.

It is possible that Joseph and Mary would have expected to be able to stay with distant relatives in Bethlehem. Extended family was important, and it would not have been unusual for a third cousin twice removed to turn up on your doorstep needing a bed for the night. But whatever their plans may have been, they didn't work out. Bethlehem must have been heaving with people that week. There wasn't even any room for them in the inn. Maybe they were allowed to shelter in the common courtyard. Or perhaps they found a crude stable somewhere. It may even have been a sort of cave, dug into the hillside for use by travellers. What did Joseph feel as a young husband unable to provide even the most basic comfort for his wife?

The conditions may not have been what Mary and Joseph had hoped for, but babies come when they are ready. So Jesus was born. Even in those difficult surroundings, it must have been special. Jesus was the Son of God, but he was also Mary's baby. She had carried him for nine months, and had laboured to bring him into the world. Try to put yourself there. For Mary and Joseph it was a unique moment in their lifetime. For us, it was the promise of the ages, fulfilled in that helpless baby.

Try to find a few moments this week to ponder this incredible story. Yahweh, God of the universe, the Sovereign Lord, had stooped to become a man. He laid aside his majesty, only to be laid in a manger. What amazing love!

'Lord, please fill me with a new sense of your amazing love today. As I realize again that Jesus' birth was a demonstration of how much you love me, help me to show your love to the children this morning in all I do and say. Amen.'

Story Time

Bible verses
Jesus was born in Bethlehem. (Matthew 2:1)
Mary laid baby Jesus in a manger. (Luke 2:7)
Joseph knew that Jesus was a special baby. (Matthew 1:21)
Mary was glad to be baby Jesus' mother. (Luke 1:48)

Birth - 2s

Mary and Joseph lived in Nazareth. Joseph had to go to a town called Bethlehem. It was nearly the time for Mary to have her baby, so she went with Joseph.

It took them a few days to get to Bethlehem. Joseph would have walked, and Mary may have ridden on a donkey. When they got to Bethlehem, there were lots and lots of people. They had to go to stay in a place that wasn't very nice.

While they were there, Mary's baby was born. His name was Jesus. Mary did not even have a bed for Jesus, so she wrapped him in some cloths and laid him on the hay in the manger. A manger is a special box where hay for the animals is kept. Mary and Joseph would have been happy that baby Jesus was born. God had told them that he would be a special baby. They loved him and wanted to look after him. They would always remember being in Bethlehem when Jesus was born.

3s - 5s

Mary and Joseph lived in a town called Nazareth. The man who was the king wanted to know how many people lived in his country, so Joseph had to go to Bethlehem to be counted. It was nearly time for Mary to have her baby, so she went with Joseph.

It took them a few days to get to Bethlehem. Joseph would have walked all the way, and Mary may have ridden on a donkey. When they got to Bethlehem there were lots and lots of people. There was no room for them in anyone's house. They had to stay in a place that wasn't very nice, perhaps a stable or a sort of cave.

While they were there, Mary's baby was born. His name was Jesus. Mary did not even have a bed for Jesus, so she wrapped him in some cloths, and laid him on the hay in the manger. A manger is a special box where hay for the animals is kept. Mary and Joseph would have been happy that baby Jesus was born. God had told them that he would be a special baby. They loved him and wanted to look after him. They would always remember being in Bethlehem when Jesus was born.

Teaching Activities

The enormity of God becoming man is hard enough for adults to comprehend - the theological details of it will, no doubt, escape the children! But what we can say to them is, 'Jesus was a special baby - God showed us he loves us when he sent Jesus.' The best teaching tools at Christmas are lives that are touched in a fresh way by the knowledge of God's love for us. We will then be able to communicate that love in action and attitude, as well as in words.

Babies

Look at Christmas books Provide one or two board books about the Christmas story. There are many available. Try to find ones with fairly realistic pictures that tell the story simply and accurately. As you show a baby the pictures, you can tell today's Bible story.

Arrange a visit from a pet For the youngest babies, a bird in a cage is probably the most appropriate visitor. They can watch the bird, and listen to it. Older babies would also enjoy a bird, or perhaps a rabbit or guinea pig. They can be helped to stroke its fur gently. Obviously, this activity isn't particularly related to the story, but it is an opportunity to enjoy the wonders of God's created world. Be natural in thanking God for the animals he has made, for ears to hear the bird sing, or for hands to feel a guinea pig's soft fur. Check with parents in advance to find out if any of the children have allergies to fur or feathers.

Play a tape of Christmas music Play a tape of instrumental Christmas music, carols or other religious Christmas music. Avoid secular Christmas music - not because there is anything wrong with it, but because we want to concentrate on the truth of the story at church.

Let older babies colour on a box Bring one or two plain, unprinted cardboard boxes. You may have to rummage around a bit at the supermarket! Provide about half a dozen chunky crayons and let older babies colour on the boxes. This will probably be a new activity for them, so you may have to guide their hands at first, until they realize that moving the crayon makes marks on the box. Again, this has little to do with the birth of baby Jesus, but it is a developmental activity. You can tell babies part of the story as they try to colour.

Toddlers

Use books about Christmas with toddlers today, as well as arranging a visit from a small pet.

Further suggestions include:
Make a footprint path around the room This idea was suggested for 2s - 3s last week. Cut out several footprints (trace around an adult shoe) and stick them on the floor with tape or Blutak. Make a path that children can walk along. The footprints should be quite close together, so you will probably need more than you think to make a good path around the room. You may need to show the children how to follow the path. As they walk on it you can tell them about Mary and Joseph going to Bethlehem. Tell as much of the story as you think they can listen to while they are walking!

Easel paint Let the children paint on easels. (You may be able to borrow some from a friendly play group or parent and toddler group.) Use red and green paint on white paper. Provide painting aprons and chunky brushes or pieces of sponge held by clothes pegs. With sponges the children can both dab and brush the paint onto the paper.

As the children paint you can sing the songs you made up for last week, or make up some new simple songs about Jesus being born. Suitable songs from 100 Action Songs for Toddlers and 100 Action Songs for Preschoolers (David C Cook Publishing Company) include 'Baby Jesus came to earth' (to the tune of 'Happy Birthday'); 'Baby Jesus sleeping on the hay'; and 'Mary rocks her baby boy' (tune of 'Mulberry Bush').

Taste cheese and raisins Bring a block of cheddar, Edam or some other mild cheese, and some raisins. Place them in a basket or on an unbreakable plate. As children come to sit with you, cut a small bit of cheese for them to taste, and let them have a few raisins. As always, watch out for the children who want to make this their lunch! You may want to talk about Mary and Joseph stopping by the side of the road to eat on their way to Bethlehem. Perhaps they had raisins or other fruit to eat. Be natural in thanking God (or even singing a thank you) for the food God gives us.

2s - 3s

Choose Christmas books to put out for the children today.

Pack a suitcase for a journey Bring a small suitcase or overnight bag, and a variety of clothing items to pack for a journey. Child-sized items will be easier for the children to manage. Pyjamas, dressing gown, trousers, shirts, and socks would be suitable. As the children pack and unpack the suitcase, you can talk about their own preparations for travelling, and about Mary and Joseph preparing for their journey to Bethlehem.

Gadget paint Provide white paper and green and red paint. Place the paint in a shallow tray and put two or three small household gadgets in each colour. A potato masher, a pastry cutter and various other items you can find around your home would be suitable. Anything that will hold paint and make an interesting pattern on the paper will work. As the children paint you may want to sing to them the Christmas songs you have made up, or tell part of the story.

Arrange a visit from a very young baby Ask the parents of the youngest baby in your church to bring their child to visit the children. Talk with the children about caring for a small baby. Although the Bible doesn't tell us, we know that Mary would have cared for Jesus in much the same way we care for our babies. Even the Son of God needed to be fed and to have his nappy changed! Help the children to understand that Mary and Joseph loved this special baby and wanted to look after him.

Cut out Christmas cards Bring a stack of old Christmas cards that you do not mind the children cutting up. There will undoubtedly be someone in the church who has a stockpile. Choose ones with realistic pictures of the manger scene, the shepherds or the wise men. Avoid secular scenes or cartoon-style pictures.

Provide children's scissors and let children cut the front off the cards, or cut out part of the pictures. Some children in this age group may have handled scissors before. For others it will be a new experience and they may need some guidance. Don't worry about what they cut out. This activity will be fun simply because children enjoy using scissors. Let those who wish take home what they have cut out.

3s - 5s

Today the 3s - 5s can use a combination of the activities for the toddlers and the 2s - 3s. They will enjoy painting at the easel with red and green paint. Tasting is always an enjoyable activity, so bring cheese and raisins as suggested for toddlers. Packing a suitcase for a journey and having a visit from a baby are appropriate activities for today.

You may also want to try the following activity:
Place animals with the bricks Bring model farm animals to put with the bricks, such as a cow, sheep, donkey and chicken. Alternatively, make animal stand-up figures. Cut out pictures of farm animals, mount them on card and cut around the shape. Glue them to cardboard tubes so that they will stand up in the brick area. Animals such as these may have been in Bethlehem when Jesus was born. You may be able to tell the story to the children as they play with the bricks and animals.

Group Time

2s - 3s

Depending on the children's level of excitement, you may need to have slightly shorter, or more active group times as Christmas approaches. Remember that today's story is one most of them will know. Tell it as accurately and simply as you can, and include other things in group time. Singing, finger plays, conversation about what the children have done during the session and prayer may all be appropriate today. As you are waiting for parents to arrive you may want to bring out any Christmas cards that were not cut up and let the children look at the pictures.

3s - 5s

Use the suggestions made for 2s - 3s. Although the children have not been cutting out cards today, you may want to bring a pile of cards with suitable pictures for the children to look through as they wait for parents to arrive. Children always seem to enjoy looking at pictures on cards.

Take Home!

JESUS IS BORN (LUKE 2:1-7)

Aim
For each child to hear an accurate account of Jesus' birth; to help the children understand that Jesus is special.

Bible verses
Jesus was born in Bethlehem. (Matthew 2:1)
Mary laid baby Jesus in a manger. (Luke 2:7)
Joseph knew that Jesus was a special baby.
(Matthew 1:21)
Mary was glad to be baby Jesus' mother.
(Luke 1:48)

The story
Mary and Joseph lived in a town called Nazareth. The man who was the king wanted to know how many people lived in his country, so Joseph had to go to Bethlehem to be counted. It was nearly time for Mary to have her baby, so she went with Joseph.

It took them a few days to get to Bethlehem. Joseph would have walked all the way, and Mary may have ridden on a donkey. When they got to Bethlehem there were lots and lots of people. There was no room for them in anyone's house. They had to stay in a place that wasn't very nice, perhaps a stable or a sort of cave.

While they were there, Mary's baby was born. His name was Jesus. Mary did not even have a bed for Jesus, so she wrapped him in some cloths, and laid him on the hay in the manger. A manger is a special box where hay for the animals is kept. Mary and Joseph would have been happy that baby Jesus was born. God had told them that he would be a special baby. They loved him and wanted to look after him. They would always remember being in Bethlehem when Jesus was born.

Activity suggestions
Look at Christmas cards together
You will probably be beginning to receive Christmas cards by now. Use this as an opportunity to talk to your baby or small child about friends and family. Even a very young baby can be shown the pictures on the front of cards. Try to take a few quiet moments several times this week to sit with your child in this way. Tell them the Bible story 'Jesus is born'. As the hectic rush of Christmas begins to heighten, these quiet moments may be good for you, as well as your child!

Pretend a journey
Talk with your child about Mary and Joseph's journey to Bethlehem and make a 'pretend' journey together. Pack a small bag of clothes and, if you have time, a small snack. Pretend you are journeying and stop along the way to eat your meal. Spread a blanket or cloth on the floor in a place where you don't usually eat! (This is a good lunchtime activity.)

Try to pretend as close to the story as you can - in other words, refrain from adding things that aren't in the Bible, like cherubs, snow, etc. We want our children to know the reality of the Christmas story, not the romanticised version that is often told.

Here Comes Christmas! week 3

PEOPLE CAME TO SEE JESUS (MATTHEW 2:1-12, LUKE 2:8-20)

Aim To help the children understand that people came to visit Jesus; they were happy he was born.

Preparation

Although their job was important, shepherds were not held in high regard by the Jews. Because of the nature of their work, they were not able to obey the many laws regarding hygiene: most of the time they were considered ceremonially unclean. They were ordinary, not particularly educated men. Isn't it interesting that they were the first ones to whom God chose to reveal the exciting news of the birth of his Son? It wasn't the 'important', socially advanced people who received this honour. It was humble men, whose hearts were open to believe. God chose the foolish things of this world to confound the wise.

When the angels had gone, the shepherds wasted no time deciding whether they were going to believe them or not. They went straight to Bethlehem. They found Mary and Joseph and baby Jesus, just as they had been told. They went away telling everyone what they had seen and what had happened to them. They were great evangelists!

What about the wise men, the Magi? Tradition has always assumed that there were three wise men because three gifts are mentioned. They were gifts such as one would bring to a king: expensive, though not very useful! It has even been suggested that Mary and Joseph may have sold the gifts to have money to live on in Bethlehem and, later, in Egypt.

By the time the wise men found him, Jesus was probably several months old. It's possible he was more than one year old. It looks nice on the Christmas cards, but the reality is that the Magi were not in the stable with the shepherds on the night of Jesus' birth. But something made them think it was worth making a great journey just to see this baby king.

If the shepherds were ordinary men, the Magi were just the opposite. And so at the beginning of Jesus' life there is a great picture of what he came to do. His cross spans every social grouping, every nationality, every intellectual level. Jesus is the one who came to break down the barriers. Bowing before Jesus, the wise men and shepherds were on level ground. In the presence of his greatness, anything of their own was worthless.

At Christmas we can learn from both the shepherds and the wise men. May God make us like the shepherds - open to believe his Word, and ready to tell everyone what we have seen and heard. And may we come to Jesus in humble worship, like the Magi, kneeling in awe and honour in his presence. That is the greatest preparation for teaching.

'Thank you, Father, for the joy and wonder of Christmas. Please help me to communicate that in every encounter with the children today. Please help me to be increasingly open to believe and act on your Word, and always ready to honour you with worship. For Jesus' sake, Amen.'

Story Time

Bible verses
The shepherds went to visit baby Jesus. (Luke 2:16)
Jesus was born in Bethlehem. (Matthew 2:1)
The shepherds were happy that baby Jesus was born. (Luke 2:20)
The wise men were glad that they could visit Jesus. (Matthew 2:11)

Birth - 2s

Mary's baby, Jesus, had been born in Bethlehem. Nearby there were some shepherds in the fields. They were looking after their sheep at night. An angel came to tell them some news: 'A special baby has been born in Bethlehem. You will be able to find him lying in a manger.' Then lots of angels came to sing about how great God is.

The shepherds went straight to Bethlehem. They found baby Jesus and Mary and Joseph. They were very happy that God had told them about Jesus.

Later on, some very wise men saw a star in the sky. They knew that a special baby had been born. They journeyed a long way to Bethlehem. They found Jesus and gave him some presents. Mary was glad that the wise men had come to see Jesus.

3s - 5s

Mary's baby, Jesus, had been born in Bethlehem. In the fields around Bethlehem there were shepherds. They were looking after their sheep at night. Suddenly, an angel came with a message from God. The shepherds were frightened. 'Don't be afraid,' the angel said. 'I have some very good news for you. A special baby has been born in Bethlehem. You will know when you find him. He is wrapped in cloths and lying in a manger.' Then, lots and lots of angels came to sing about how great God is.

When the angels had gone, the shepherds went straight to Bethlehem. They found baby Jesus with Mary and Joseph. The shepherds were very happy that God had told them about Jesus.

Later on some very wise men saw a star in the sky. They knew it meant that a special baby had been born. They wanted to see the baby. They journeyed a long way to Bethlehem. At last they found Jesus. They gave him some presents. Mary was glad that the wise men had come to see Jesus.

Teaching Activities

Older under fives are likely to know a fair bit about today's Bible story. In fact, they may know some 'extras' that they have picked up along the way. As always, we must be true to what the Bible says, avoiding our own additions and subtractions, as well as communicating the humanity of the people in its stories. Let's try to help all the children understand that many people were very happy that Jesus was born.

Babies

Look at Christmas baubles Put one or two shiny plastic Christmas tree decorations in a clear plastic container for babies to look at. You could also make a mobile by hanging three or four from a coat hanger; babies will watch the baubles as they reflect the light. Talk to the babies about Christmas being a happy time, then tell them about people who came to see Jesus.

Make a Christmas design book Use sturdy card to make a book of Christmas patterns. Glue Christmas ribbon (with the ends dangling loose), and various circles, squares or triangles of wrapping paper on each page. Try to avoid pictures of Father Christmas, reindeer, elves etc. Robins and bells are acceptable! As you show a baby the bright colours you can communicate the joy of Christmas.

Make music with bells If you have a set of children's instruments you may already have some bells. Otherwise, you may be able to buy a few in a craft shop. You can sew them onto a wide piece of elastic, then make it into a wristband. A baby can hold it, or you can slide it onto his or her wrist. As a baby jingles the bells you can sing the Christmas songs that you have made up, as well as thanking God for ears to hear. (Supervise carefully so that babies do not put bells into their mouths.)

Make a coloured torch Obtain two ordinary household torches and some green and red cellophane or acetate with which to cover the light. Secure with tape or an elastic band. Shine coloured light on the wall or ceiling, or even inside the hood of a pram if the baby is lying down and awake. As with most of this unit's activities, this is not connected directly with the story, but all activities have the baby's developmental process in mind. Enabling them to experience something when they hear a teacher say, 'Thank you, God, for eyes to see colours' helps them, over time, to make these links for themselves. They begin to understand that God gave them eyes.

Toddlers
Toddlers will enjoy the red and green coloured torches. You can shine them on the ceiling, or you could bring in a fairly large cardboard box to shine them into so the children can see the different colours clearly.

Additional activities include:
Add farm animals to the bricks This activity was suggested for 3s - 5s last week. You can talk about the animals that may have been around when Jesus was born, particularly donkeys and sheep. As children play with the animals and bricks, you can tell part of the story, especially about the shepherds.

Glue a collage of ribbons and wrappings Provide a variety of circles, squares and triangles of Christmas wrapping paper, using the same cautions as given for the babies' book of Christmas designs. Cut 12 cm lengths of coloured ribbon. Let each child glue a collage of colourful Christmas wrappings. (It may make the ribbon easier to stick down if you curl one end with scissors. The children then need only glue the straight end to their paper.) This will be a fun activity and in the lively atmosphere you can talk about the joy of the shepherds and the wise men.

Use playdough in the home corner Bring playdough to put in the home corner. You may also want to bring rolling pins and shape cutters, but as most toddlers can't manage them without help, it might be better to provide only dough, so that whatever they do will be their own unaided work. They can play with playdough on its own, or put it in the dishes and pans as 'food'.

2s - 3s
You can put farm animals with the bricks for 2s and 3s today. They will also enjoy the coloured torches. If you can darken the room without frightening the children, they may enjoy taking turns shining the torches onto the ceiling. Otherwise, they can shine them into a box.

Other activities include:
Taste cheese and raisins You can use this activity in exactly the same way as suggested for the 3s - 5s last week.

Easel paint This activity can also be used just as it was last week for 3s - 5s.

Wrap parcels Bring in several small empty cardboard boxes. Provide inexpensive wrapping paper (again, choose designs as carefully as you can), scissors and clear tape. Help the children 'wrap' parcels for Christmas. Provide ribbons and bows if you wish. Most children will be happy just wrapping the paper on the boxes. Don't worry about final results. Try to let the children do as much as possible by themselves. When all boxes have been wrapped and other children want a turn, let them tear the paper off the boxes and start again. As you do this activity it will be natural to talk about the wise men bringing presents to Jesus.

3s - 5s
Children are fascinated by torches, so use the coloured light activity. Wrapping parcels should prove to be popular, and let the children make collages as suggested for toddlers.

Two other ideas are:

Have a visit from a pet You may be able to arrange for a return appearance by the pet that visited the toddlers last week, or you may be able to 'borrow' a hamster, gerbil or rabbit from someone else. Not every activity you use has to have a direct link with the teaching aim. It is good to introduce nature activities every few weeks to help children grow in their understanding that God made the world. Remember to check with parents regarding allergies to fur and feathers.

Make a set of 'fuzzy felts' Obtain sheets of felt in a variety of colours. Cut out a simple Christmas tree shape from green felt, about 30 cm high. Use the other colours to cut small circles, triangles, bells and stars to place on the tree as decorations. Let the children decorate and redecorate the tree as much as they want. You could even cut slightly larger squares to use as packages under the tree.

As children play with the felts you can talk about the people they will visit, or have a visit from, at Christmas. Talk also about the people who came to see Jesus.

Group Time

2s - 3s

It might be helpful to burn off some of the children's energy as they come to group time today. You could play 'follow the leader' and lead them around the room with simple actions such as marching, waving arms, jumping, etc. Then, as they sit in the circle, you could use one or two simple finger plays to settle their smaller muscles. Tell the story early on in group time while they are still able to concentrate. When you have finished talking, singing and praying, you could take turns rolling a ball to one another as you wait for parents to arrive.

3s - 5s

As with the two and three-year-olds, you may want to start group time with 'follow the leader' and some finger plays. This age group should be able to concentrate for longer, but it may still be a good idea to tell the story early in group time. If possible, talk to the children about the session's activities, sing some songs, and let them pray. If not, use group time today for more active things. You could roll a ball or toss a beanbag as you wait for parents.

Playdough – a basic recipe

1 cup of salt
2 cups of flour
2 tablespoons cooking oil or baby oil
2 teaspoons cream of tartar
2 cups of water
a few drops of food colouring

Mix all the ingredients in a saucepan. Cook over a medium heat, stirring continuously. The mixture will form a consistency similar to scrambled eggs and will start to come away from the side of the pan. A lump will form. Remove from heat, allow to cool and knead on a clean surface. Store in an airtight box or polythene bag. Keep in a cool place.

Take Home!

PEOPLE CAME TO SEE JESUS
(MATTHEW 2:1-12, LUKE 2:8-20)

Aim
To help the children understand that people came to visit Jesus; they were happy he was born.

Bible verses
The shepherds went to visit baby Jesus.
(Luke 2:16)
Jesus was born in Bethlehem. (Matthew 2:1)
The shepherds were happy that baby Jesus was born. (Luke 2:20)
The wise men were glad that they could visit Jesus. (Matthew 2:11)

The story
Mary's baby, Jesus, had been born in Bethlehem. In the fields around Bethlehem there were shepherds. They were looking after their sheep at night. Suddenly, an angel came with a message from God. The shepherds were frightened. 'Don't be afraid,' the angel said. 'I have some very good news for you. A special baby has been born in Bethlehem. You will know when you find him. He is wrapped in cloths and lying in a manger.' Then, lots and lots of angels came to sing about how great God is.

When the angels had gone, the shepherds went straight to Bethlehem. They found baby Jesus with Mary and Joseph. The shepherds were very happy that God had told them about Jesus.

Later on some very wise men saw a star in the sky. They knew it meant that a special baby had been born. They wanted to see the baby. They journeyed a long way to Bethlehem. At last they found Jesus. They gave him some presents. Mary was glad that the wise men had come to see Jesus.

Activity suggestions
Make a Christmas design book
Use thick card to make a book of Christmas patterns. Glue squares, circles and triangles of colourful wrapping paper on each page; glue in some Christmas ribbon as well (curl the ends with scissors if you wish). Cut out appropriate pictures from old Christmas cards. Make the book for your baby and tell him or her about the shepherds and the wise men as you look at it. If you have an older under five, you can work together to make the book.

Wrap parcels
If possible, let your child help you wrap the Christmas presents. Alternatively give him / her a couple of empty boxes and some re-cycled wrapping paper to pretend with. You could even let them make their own wrapping paper by decorating scrap paper with crayons, felt tips or stickers. As you do this together, tell your child about the shepherds and wise men. Talk about giving presents as a way of showing people that we love them. God showed us his love when he sent his son, Jesus.

Here Comes Christmas! week 4

BABY JESUS GOES TO CHURCH (LUKE 2:21-39)

Aim For children to learn that Jesus went to church when he was a baby; that people at church were glad to see Jesus.

Preparation

Jewish law declared a woman unclean after childbirth. After the allotted time had passed (about six weeks), the woman was to present herself and her firstborn son at the Temple, along with a sacrifice. So Mary and Joseph took Jesus on the eight-mile journey to Jerusalem to fulfil the Law.

The Temple was huge, and always buzzing with people. Somehow, God led Simeon to the right young couple. What a moment that must have been for him! Before him lay the promised One, God's anointed Messiah. He took Jesus in his arms and praised the Lord. The gist of his prayer was, 'Sovereign Lord, you are absolutely incredible! This is what I have been waiting for. I can die happy now, because you have fulfilled your promise' (Luke 2:28-32).

Then Simeon turned his attention to Mary and Joseph. They were already astonished by what he had said about Jesus. Now he had some strange and not-so-positive words for them. At the beginning of your child's life you don't exactly want to hear that he will cause the rising and falling of many, that he will be spoken against and that, because of him, a sword will pierce your own soul. Mary and Joseph must have been reeling from their encounter with Simeon.

They had no time to recover, though, for at the next moment Anna appeared. She, too, was very godly. She had been a widow for many years, and rather than becoming embittered by this fact, she had devoted her life to a ministry of prayer. She, like Simeon, was looking forward to the coming Messiah. So when she saw Mary and Joseph with the baby Jesus, and heard Simeon's words, she was thrilled. She gave thanks to God.

What a day for Mary and Joseph! They must have talked it over a hundred times in the weeks, even years, that followed. Their hearts would have been thrilled with the initial words and blessings from Simeon and Anna. But what did Mary carry around with her all those years concerning Simeon's later words? Only at the cross did she fully understand what he had meant when he said a sword would pierce her soul.

Despite these concerns, this must have been an overwhelmingly joyful day for this new family. Pretty good for a first trip to church with your new baby!

Let's ask God to teach us from the example of Simeon and Anna. Because they were both so close to God, they were able to be in the right place at the right time. What a thrill to know you are seeing God's purposes worked out before your very eyes! And that can be true in our lives as well. We can see God working out his purpose for us and for others as we seek to be holy and devote our lives to knowing God.

'Please help me today, Lord, to be genuinely glad that each child has come to church. Please give me extra love and patience for those children who are difficult, or who are simply excited because it is Christmas time. As I teach today, fill me with a joy I can share with the children and their parents. I pray in Jesus' precious name, Amen.'

Story Time

Bible verses
God loved us and sent his Son. (John 3:16)
Baby Jesus went to church with Mary and Joseph. (Luke 2:22)
Simeon was glad to see baby Jesus. (Luke 2:28)
Anna was glad that baby Jesus was at church. (Luke 2:38)

Birth - 2s
When Jesus was still a tiny baby, Joseph and Mary took him to the big church in Jerusalem. There was a man called Simeon who loved God very much. He had been waiting a long time to see the special one who was God's Son. When he saw baby Jesus, he was very happy. 'This is what I have been waiting for,' he said. 'This is a special baby sent from God.'

There was also a woman named Anna at the big church that day. When she saw Simeon with the baby Jesus, Mary and Joseph, she was very happy. She said thank you to God for Jesus. She told lots of people about the special baby she had seen.

3s - 5s
When Jesus was still a tiny baby, Joseph and Mary took him to the big church in Jerusalem. They wanted to say thank you to God for baby Jesus. There was a man called Simeon who loved God very much. He had been waiting for a long time to see the one who was God's son. He went to the big church in Jerusalem that day, too. When he saw baby Jesus, he was very happy. 'I know that this is what I have been waiting for,' he said. 'This is the special one that God promised to send.'

There was a woman named Anna at the big church that day. She also loved God very much. When she saw Simeon with baby Jesus, Mary and Joseph, she was very happy. She said thank you to God for Jesus. She told lots of other people about the baby she had seen.

Teaching Activities

Mary and Joseph must have been glad that they took Jesus to church that day. Let's pray that each family represented by the children we teach will be glad they have come to church today. Simeon and Anna were pleased to see Jesus at the Temple. Let's show each child we teach that we are pleased they are here today.

Babies
Play a tape of Christmas music If possible use a different tape from the one used two weeks ago.

Play with toy animals Bring some toy animals for babies to play with. Make sure they are big enough and tough enough to withstand a baby's mouth. You may also want to bring a selection of farm animals. You can talk about the animals that may have been involved in the Christmas story.

Make a stacking toy with tins Wash and remove the labels from a variety of empty tins that will stack together. This an inexpensive alternative to buying a set of stackers. If you are concerned about the noise as one tin drops into another, cut circles of felt to size, and glue one to the base of each tin. As you stack the tins for the babies, tell them that you are glad they are at church today. Sing 'I am happy, I am happy, you're at church today.' Tell babies about Simeon and Anna being glad to see baby Jesus.

Make 'bricks' from boxes Cover some small cardboard boxes in silver foil, or red or green foil wrapping paper to make 'bricks'. They won't be very sturdy, but they should last the session. The bright shiny surface will catch a baby's eye. Half a dozen bricks will be enough. As you stack them for a baby to push over, you can talk about baby Jesus going to church.

Toddlers

Make foil-covered bricks from boxes and a set of stacking tins for toddlers.

Some other ideas include:

Water paint a box Bring a medium-sized cardboard box (two if you have several toddlers) for the children to paint with water. Put a small amount of water into spill-proof paint pots, and provide chunky paint brushes. Refill the pots as necessary. The children can sit on the floor to 'paint', or you can put the box on a low table. You may want to use painting aprons if you are concerned that the children might get a bit soggy! As they paint, sing to the children or talk to them about happy things we do at church. Tell them about baby Jesus going to church.

Play bells and triangles Look through your collection of musical instruments and find some triangles and sets of bells. Let the children play them, either sitting or walking round the room. It's likely that you may only want to use this activity for a few minutes at a time. Supervise this activity carefully so that the children do not hurt themselves with the triangle beaters.

Colour with red, green and blue crayons Provide red, green and blue chunky crayons for the children to use. Make the activity a little bit different by cutting white drawing paper into large circles or triangles. As children colour, tell them part of the Bible story - if they are able to listen and colour at the same time! As they finish their pictures and you put them to one side, you could say something like: 'You have coloured a picture today at church, Sarah. It is nice to come to church. Jesus went to church when he was a baby.' Although this statement seems very simplistic to adult ears, it helps young children link what they are doing with where they are.

Blow bubbles This may be an activity you want to save until the end while you are waiting for parents. Let the children try to catch the bubbles as you blow them, but keep an eye open for children who may bump into one another! If there are two adults, one can blow bubbles while the other sings songs about coming to church - for example, 'This is the way we go to church', no 39 in *100 Action Songs for Preschoolers*, David C Cook Publishing Company.

2s - 3s

We will look at a whole new set of activities for the two and three-year-olds today. Some of them are taken from ideas used with toddlers and 3s - 5s last week.

Arrange a visit from a pet If all the groups have been borrowing the same pet, it will have become more regular in its attendance than some church members! The information you need for this activity is in the 3s - 5s section of Week 3 and the Babies section of Week 2.

Make a collage of ribbons and wrappings Toddlers and 3s - 5s used this art activity last week. If possible make use of any left-over scraps of ribbon and wrapping paper. As the children look at the various patterns, pictures and words on the wrapping paper you can talk to them about Simeon and Anna being glad to see baby Jesus at church. Most children are delighted when an adult calls them by name and says 'I'm glad you came to church today.'

Use animals in sand play Last week you put animals with the bricks. Bring them again today and put them in sand, using a washing-up bowl or an old baby bath as a container. Put a large plastic sheet or lots of newspaper under the sand area to make cleaning-up easier. As children play with the animals in the sand, you can talk about animals that may have featured in any of the stories used in this Christmas unit. Supervise carefully so that the children do not throw the sand or put it in their mouths.

Sort buttons If you do not have your own 'button box', try to find a person who does - perhaps someone at church who knits or sews. Collect about six or seven buttons in each of four colours for the children to sort. The greater the variety of shapes and sizes, the better. Place the buttons in a container, and provide a container with compartments for sorting them into. An egg box or a bun tin are suitable. Children may need help in sorting: the buttons are bound to be different shades of a colour. This activity promotes colour recognition and eye-hand co-ordination.

3s - 5s

Sorting buttons should be fun for this group today. You may be able to provide more buttons in a greater variety of colours for these slightly older children. Bring the fuzzy felts you made for last time and let the children use them again.

Other activities you can use include:

Easel paint Young children rarely tire of painting at an easel, so this activity can be used again. Let the children paint with white paint on red or green paper. For variety, cut the paper into a large circle, or an irregular shape. Put white paint in three different pots and provide three sizes of brush - narrow, medium and very chunky. The children can then vary the detail of their pictures. As you talk and sing about painting and other fun things we do at church, you can tell part of the Bible story.

Make puzzles from Christmas cards Choose three or four old Christmas cards with suitable pictures and make puzzles from them. You may want to make them slightly more robust by gluing them onto slightly thicker card. Cut each card into three or four pieces, making sure they are not too difficult to fit back together. Put them out in a box lid or on a tray for children to work. They may want to tell you about Christmas cards they have received. As you talk about fun things related to Christmas, tell them about how happy Simeon and Anna were when they saw baby Jesus at church.

Make Christmas cards Let the children make Christmas cards to send. You may want to suggest a recipient: parent, grandparent or friend. Provide A4 sheets of blue paper, folded in half. On the inside of each card, glue a square of white paper for the message. Let the children decorate the card with silver and gold stickers, or silver and gold glitter glue. Ask each child to tell you for whom they want to make their card, and what they want you to write inside. Some children may need a little guidance. 'Happy Christmas' is perfectly adequate if that is all they want to say. Let those who can, write their own name. You may be able to talk to the children about giving. We give to others at Christmas to say that we love them. God loved us and sent his Son.

Group Time

2s - 3s

As the children come to group time you may want to show them the visiting pet and let them look at it once again and talk about how to care for it, about its food and so on. When you have finished discussing it, put the animal out of sight so the children can concentrate as you tell the Bible story. As you wait for parents to arrive you can blow bubbles for the children to catch.

3s - 5s

You may want to call the children to group time by singing their names today. Have them stand in a corner of the room. Sit on the mat and call them one at a time by singing, 'I am happy, I am happy, (Name) is here today.' As you tell the story about Simeon and Anna being glad to see Jesus, the children will be pleased to know that you are glad they, too, came to church.

As you wait for parents to arrive, you can blow bubbles for the children to catch. If you have a fairly large group, you may need to name three or four children at a time to catch the bubbles. One teacher can sit with the others, while a few children have their turn.

Take Home!

BABY JESUS GOES TO CHURCH
(LUKE 2:21-39)

Aim
For children to learn that Jesus went to church when he was a baby; that people at church were glad to see Jesus.

Bible verses
God loved us and sent his Son. (John 3:16)
Baby Jesus went to church with Mary and Joseph. (Luke 2:22)
Simeon was glad to see baby Jesus. (Luke 2:28)
Anna was glad that baby Jesus was at church. (Luke 2:38)

The story
When Jesus was still a tiny baby, Joseph and Mary took him to the big church in Jerusalem. They wanted to say thank you to God for baby Jesus. There was a man called Simeon who loved God very much. He had been waiting for a long time to see the one who was God's son. He went to the big church in Jerusalem that day, too. When he saw baby Jesus, he was very happy. 'I know that this is what I have been waiting for,' he said. 'This is the special one that God promised to send.'

There was a woman named Anna at the big church that day. She also loved God very much. When she saw Simeon with baby Jesus, Mary and Joseph, she was very happy. She said thank you to God for Jesus. She told lots of other people about the baby she had seen.

Activity suggestions
Blow bubbles
Christmas can be an overwhelming time for babies and young children - and for their parents. Any normal routine seems to go out of the window. Try to find a few quiet moments with just you and your child. Blow bubbles for your baby to watch, and for an older child to catch. (Sometimes you can snatch these moments of peace when your baby / child is in the bath.)

As you enjoy some time together, tell your baby or older under five about Jesus going to church.

Make puzzles from Christmas cards
Choose three or four old Christmas cards with suitable pictures and make puzzles from them. You may want to make them slightly more robust by gluing them onto thicker card. Cut each card into three or four pieces, making sure they are not too difficult to fit back together. As you and your child play with the puzzles, talk about fun things related to Christmas and tell him / her about how happy Simeon and Anna were when they saw baby Jesus at church.